INFLATION

INFLATION

CAUSES,
CONSEQUENCES,
and CURES

George W. Wilson

INDIANA UNIVERSITY PRESS
BLOOMINGTON

Library of Congress Cataloging in Publication Data
Wilson, George Wilton, 1928–
    Inflation—causes, consequences, and cures.
    Includes bibliographical references and index.
    1. Inflation (Finance) I. Title.
HG229.W55 332.4'1 81–47830 AACR2
ISBN 0–253–33008–4
ISBN 0–253–20277–9 (pbk.)   1 2 3 4 5 86 85 84 83 82

To Marie, Ron, Doug, and Suzanne,
as always

Contents

Preface

This book is directed toward that elusive animal often referred to as "the intelligent layman." Therefore, it presupposes no prior knowledge of the dismal science known as economics. Accordingly, I have eschewed the use of equations and graphs as explanatory tools (with a few minor exceptions). There are several tables, charts, and numbers, since economics does deal with quantities and their interrelationships. But I have tried to present in literary and understandable form what economists in general know about inflation—its causes, consequences, and cures.

Inflation is obviously of great concern not only in the United States but throughout the world. It has often been dubbed "public enemy number one" by presidents, prime ministers, and other heads of state. Yet in the late 1960s, the 1970s, and the early 1980s, a reasonable resolution of the malady has not been achieved. Various approaches ranging from outright price controls to tight money, balanced budgets, and deliberate creation of recessions have been tried without success. The public is understandably confused. I hope the present volume contributes to a better comprehension of this phenomenon, why it is so difficult to contain, and the trade-offs involved in making such attempts.

I have been advised by various readers of the manuscript that, while it does not grip like Phillip Roth or 007, it can be read. Some have even said they learned something from it. No greater compliment could be paid to one who "professes" to know something about this subject.

This is not a textbook, although some courses in economics may find it a useful supplement. My aim throughout has been to be understood by concerned and reasonably intelligent laymen (and women). We need all the help we can get in this troubled and uncertain world. I hope this volume helps.

I wish to thank Bradford Richardson for helping with the materials on Brazilian and German inflation in chapter 2 and for his suggestions throughout. An unknown reader also provided useful advice.

INFLATION

1 Introduction

Inflation is like the weather: Everyone talks about it but no one does anything about it. Like the weather, which is thus far beyond our control, we can take certain defensive measures to offset the impacts of inflation just as we build shelters with heat or cooling devices to escape the consequences of inclemency. However, unlike the weather, inflation is a man-made phenomenon. Unless the genie has been let out of the bottle, what man has created should be amenable to control or prevention. Instead of passive acquiescence to the inevitability of inflation, as with a thunderstorm, it should be possible not only to moderate its effects but to prevent it altogether.

Yet most economies in the Western world have not had much success since 1965 in dealing with inflation. Two U.S. presidents (Ford and Carter) have referred to it as "public enemy number one." Inflation remains a matter of substantial concern because of its seeming inevitability, persistence, and apparent immunity to numerous remedies, except at "unacceptable" social costs. Savants in the profession of economics and numerous politicians have produced a bewildering variety of answers, none of which has gained unequivocal acceptance. The public is therefore concerned with causes, consequences, and cures for inflation. The weather is tolerated because we are helpless to control it; inflation is not, because it is (or is thought to be) controllable—at least within limits more tolerable than in recent experience.

This volume will examine some past historical inflationary episodes, the various apparent causes of inflation, its consequences, and possible cures. Let us begin with a definition of inflation.

Inflation has often been defined as "too much money chasing too few goods." This, however, is more an explanation of inflation than a definition, attributing the cause of inflation to monetary growth relative to the output of goods and services. What *is* inflation? It is a *persistent* rise in the *general* level of prices. A specific price may rise dramatically as in the case of oil or gas. But if the specific price is offset by declines in other prices, the *general* price level may not rise at all. Nor will the dramatic rise necessarily be followed by further increases. We are immediately faced with the problem of defining the terms "general price level" and "persistent." Since the general level of prices depends on a series of individual price changes and their relative importance, we clearly require some measure of these factors, namely, a price index.

But a one- or two-point rise in some price index would not constitute what is generally meant by inflation, nor would its consequences be particularly serious if the change in the price index quickly reversed itself and price stability ensued. People ride out temporary storms. Thus, inflation means more than a single rise in a price index. To become and remain a problem warranting concern, inflation must involve a long succession of increases in a price index. How long is "long" in a monthly or annual sense is not something amenable to calculation. Intuitively, however, when inflation (defined as a succession of monthly or annual increases in a price index or all price indexes) persists so long that the principal economic actors in the economy believe it will continue, that will define "long" or "persistent." Clearly, this cannot be measured precisely. Whether years or months of increase in a price index is necessary to change expectations from those of price stability to continued price rises will depend on one's perception of current and likely future events. At the moment (1981), the anticipated increases in defense spending, as a result of Soviet expansion into Afghanistan and Mr. Reagan's election, will probably increase the Federal Government budget. And this increase, on top of many years of higher-than-usual price increases, will accentuate inflationary expectations. On the other hand, inflation expectations will be reduced if the economy sinks into recession in 1981. We shall see that the revision of expectations up or down is an important determinant of inflation. To this extent inflation is in part self-generating and self-reinforcing, once begun.

Inflation, then, as a serious problem, is closely related to inflation expectations. And these are even more closely related to past rates of inflation and to current and anticipated conditions—political, social, as well as economic. Furthermore, inflation may involve "steady state" inflation, in which the appropriate price index or indexes increase by about the same proportion per year (e.g., 5% or 15%), or at an accelerating rate (e.g., 2% in period 1, 5% in period 2, 8% in period 3, etc.) or at a decelerating rate (e.g., 10% in period 1, 8% in period 2, 6% in period 3, etc.) or at a varying rate (e.g., 8% in period 1, 5% in period 2, 10% in period 3, etc.). Each of these patterns will condition future expectations differently in addition to the length of time each has persisted as well as contemporary circumstances.

There is another aspect of defining inflation as something more than a steady increase in a price index. For example, in the United States the Consumer Price Index (CPI) rose every year from 1950 through 1967 (except 1955). Yet inflation was not considered serious, largely because the increases in the CPI were mostly under 2% per year (except for the short-lived buying spree in 1951 induced by the Korean War). Indeed, the annual change varied erratically within a relatively narrow range of 1%–4%, exhibiting no strong upward trend. This was widely viewed as acceptable or decent price behavior. Thus, so long as the rate of change of a price index stays within acceptable bounds, and bounds to which society has become accustomed, while there is inflation in the technical sense of a persistent rise in the price index, it does not cause much alarm or many perceptible difficulties.

For inflation to be taken as a serious social and economic problem, a price index's rate of change must take a fairly sharp upward jump over some previous norm or accustomed level—a jump that either continues to accelerate or that remains at the new higher level. From 1967 on, the CPI has increased at rates well above 4% (except for 1972), and the rate of increase has risen steadily during the last four years—from roughly 6% per year in 1976 to over 13% in 1979 and 1980.

Thus we may define inflation as a sharp increase in the rate of change of some price index above a previous normal level that persists over a time period long enough to revise upward expectations of its future persistence. This is the sense I believe most people have of the "inflation problem" in the U.S. in the 1970s and 1980s.

We have used the term "price index" and specifically the "CPI" in defining inflation. Given the widespread use of price indexes and the apparently widespread misunderstanding of them, it is useful at the outset to provide a better understanding of them.

What Is a Price Index?

A price index is a weighted average of the prices of a predetermined basket or collection of commodities. Its level is usually related to some "base" year or period and arbitrarily defined as 100.0 for that year. Thus, when the Consumer Price Index is estimated to be 217.4 for the year 1979 as a whole, this means that on the average during 1979 it would cost $217.40 to purchase the same quantities of goods that in 1967 (the base year) cost $100.00.

More important than the *level* of the index at any particular time is the rate of change in the index from period to period. A price index change is merely a weighted average of individual price changes in an economy. In a market-oriented economy, many prices change daily, weekly, or yearly in response to the changing conditions of supply or demand. An excess of supply over demand at a given price will lead, sooner or later, to a price reduction. When this occurs the quantities people choose to put on the market equal the quantities others want to buy at that price. Similarly, an excess demand will raise the price. The extent and speed of such price adjustments depend on the institutional arrangements and market structure in specific instances. But over long enough periods, chronic conditions of excess supply (demand) will lead to either price decreases (increases) in particular markets or withdrawal (increase) of supply. In highly competitive markets, the adjustment is largely in terms of price in the short run, while in less competitive markets, the adjustment to an excess supply will usually be an output reduction.

I shall discuss these issues of structure and institutional arrangements in particular markets in more detail later, since they become important influences in the process of inflation. At this point, I merely want to stress that in any market-oriented economy specific prices naturally tend to change frequently. A price index is thus a proxy measure of the general level of prices that seeks to measure the change in selected specific prices and to weight this in terms of the relative importance of these commodities.

The problem is, Which prices should be selected as indicators of the "general level of prices" and how assign the weights? Assume a simple economy with only three goods—A, B, and C—whose prices in some time period are P_A, P_B, and P_C. Suppose in some subsequent time period all three prices are found to have risen by 10%. It would then be legitimate to conclude that the general level of prices had risen by 10% and that the rate of inflation was 10%. But it never happens that all prices rise or fall by precisely the same proportions. What if P_A rose by 10%, P_B by 5%, and P_C by 20%? It would still be accurate to say that the general level of prices had increased. However, the actual rate of inflation would be more conjectural.

Similarly, assume P_A rose by 10%, P_B *decreased* by 15%, and P_C remained constant. What would be the percentage change in the general level of prices or the rate of inflation? Clearly, the answer depends on the relative importance of the three commodities. If we know the *quantities* of the three commodities purchased at a particular time, we may determine the relative importance, in terms of expenditures, of each. Thus, if it is found in some period that the total expenditures of a particular person or group (e.g., urban wage earners) were 30% on commodity A, 20% on B, and 50% on C, we could use these as weights to determine the change in overall prices.

In the last example, if P_A rose by 10% and its relative importance were 30%, this would raise the overall or general level of prices by 3%. Since P_B decreased by 15% and its relative importance was 20%, this alone would lower the overall level of prices by 3%. If P_C remained constant, the overall percentage change in prices would be zero % (i.e., +3%, −3%, +0%).

The measurement of inflation thus involves selecting a set of prices of "representative" commodities in "representative" regions, determining a set of weights, and then deducing the weighted sum of the percentage changes in each price from period to period.

There are many ways to determine representative prices, using fixed "base period" weights (à la the CPI) or shifting weights per period (à la the GNP deflator). It is not easy to account for significant shifts in people's spending patterns, or to account for new products, quality changes, or regional changes. Thus the *measurement* of inflation by one or more price indexes is clearly imperfect.

Yet beginning in the middle to late 1960s, all the available price indexes began shifting to much higher levels than existed before (see table 3.2). They have continued to grow at higher-than-usual levels, with one or two exceptions, on an annual basis, and all have reached virtually new plateaus as the U.S. economy enters the decade of the 1980s. Inflation rates, however measured, are widely viewed as "too high" and little improvement is expected in the near future.

The recent experience and future outlook thus raise three major issues: (1) What causes inflation? (2) What are the consequences of inflation? and (3) What can or should be done about it—the cures? Before attempting to answer these questions directly, it will be useful and informative to examine inflationary experiences past and present.

2 Inflation Historically Revisited

SECULAR INFLATION

Inflationary phenomena have been evident ever since the first widespread use of money to replace the cumbersome barter system. Inflationary episodes usually accompanied war, sudden changes in population due to famine or pestilence (e.g., the Black Death of the fourteenth century), periods of scarcity due to poor crops, debasement of the coinage, or sudden influxes of the monetary substance (gold, silver, copper, for example). Obviously, there are no reliable price indexes nor much in the way of economic data as we now think of it. Yet there is evidence, for example, that sharp increases in wages and prices occurred in ancient Greece following Alexander the Great's conquest of Persia in 330 B.C. which led to large inflows of Persian gold into the Greek economy. The later Roman Empire seemed especially susceptible to monetary instability as well as to severe inflationary pressures. It is therefore not surprising that one of the first "price control" schemes for which we have evidence is the Edict of Diocletian (301 A.D.). The edict fixed maximum prices throughout the empire for "all the necessaries and commodities of life"[1] including ceiling prices on oil, salt, honey, meat, poultry, game, fish, vegetables, fruit, wages of laborers, artisans, schoolmasters and orators, clothes, harness, timber, corn, wine, and beer. In all, price ceilings were imposed on over 900 commodities and 130 grades of labor. The inflation rate had been very high during the preceding century. Butcher's meat, for example, more than quadrupled in price. The price fixed by the edict was exactly four times what it had been in the second century.[2] The price of wheat is estimated to have risen 200 times over the century and a half preceding the edict.[3] The death penalty was imposed on both buyer and seller for transactions above the maximum. The edict was in force until 305 A.D., during which time numerous death sentences were handed out, labor market disturbances occurred, and some products disappeared from the market.[4] There is no evidence to indicate that this early attempt at comprehensive wage-price controls was a success.

The next inflationary surge for which there is reasonably good evidence did not occur until the sixteenth century. Data after the fall of Rome in the fifth century until the sixteenth century are at best spotty and usually nonexistent—at least until about the thirteenth century, except for a few selected regions in western Europe.[5] What the few statistics on prices show for England and France is low average annual rates of price increase: less than 2% between 1326–50 and 1351–75, small annual rates of decrease (about 1%) between 1351–75 and 1376–1400, and price stability from 1376–1400 to 1476–1500.[6] Parts of Spain (Aragon and Navarre) had somewhat higher rates of inflation (above 2%) during the early period, with Aragon following the English and French patterns for the latter two periods. Navarre, however, sustained its relatively high inflation rate until 1400.

The comparatively low rate of inflation—at least in England in the early period—however, masks a dramatic event that occurred between 1347 and 1350, namely, the Black Death or bubonic plague, "the most horrible of all epidemics mentioned in history."[7] It is estimated to have killed almost one-third of the population in England as well as in the rest of western Europe, across which it spread. The impact was dramatic on wages; they appear to have doubled in England (and probably elsewhere) between 1347 and 1350. Despite legislation to hold wages down, a new wage plateau had apparently been reached. The impact on overall prices was far less. "Food prices on the average rose very little" and were "remarkably stable for a century or more after 1350,"[8] although with plenty of severe year-to-year fluctuations, depending on locale. However, nonfood prices rose comparably to the cost of labor, especially for those products in which more labor per unit of output was required. This short-run inflation episode is averaged out when using a base year average of prices extending from 1326 to 1350.

The Sixteenth-century Price "Revolution"

The term "revolution" frequently used by historians of western Europe seems a bit strong if we confine our attention solely to the rate of price increase throughout the sixteenth century and first half of the seventeenth. Over this long period, the rate of increase of key prices and groups of prices barely averaged, by most measures, 1% annually and certainly below 2%.[9] This is a pretty tame affair compared with modern standards. Yet it was the longest reasonably sustained inflation ever recorded and the first after which prices did not descend to their beginning level. A new price plateau had been reached (see figure 2.1), from which

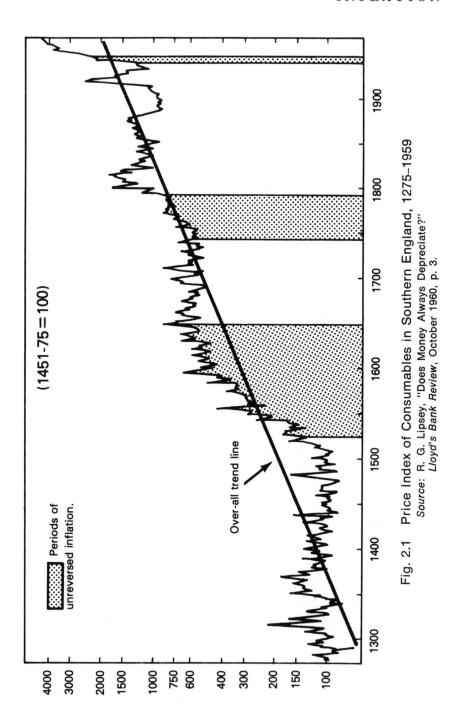

Fig. 2.1   Price Index of Consumables in Southern England, 1275–1959
Source: R. G. Lipsey, "Does Money Always Depreciate?"
Lloyd's Bank Review, October 1960, p. 3.

subsequent inflations or inflationary epochs took off. Furthermore, those experiencing it expressed alarm at the "high price of things." Jean Bodin, in France, talks about the "advance in price of everything" and even estimates that wines and grains cost "twenty times as much as they did a hundred years ago."[10] In England, John Hales was especially concerned with high prices and sought, as did Bodin, to provide an explanation of the inflation and suggest remedies. Contemporary sentiment, in short, sensed that something new and inexplicable was happening.

And indeed it was. The erosion of the last vestiges of feudal institutions was vastly accelerated as "traditional" prices gave way to market-determined prices and the economy became a larger, interrelated unit rendering the manorial system obsolete. The pace of inflation fluctuated sharply from year to year and from place to place. The most dramatic episode for England was associated with the "Great Debasement" between 1543 and 1551, which "caused widespread hardship, confusion and discontent."[11] A glance at figure 2.1 indicates a very sharp rise in the price index during this period of almost 300%. The cause of this episode is usually ascribed to serious debasement of the English coinage by the Tudor kings, but especially by Henry VIII (1509–1547) and his immediate successor.[12] The sudden increase in the money supply, coupled with the economic dislocation associated with the Enclosure Movement, Henry VIII's extravagances, and constant warfare, probably account for this sharp break with traditional prices and price relationships.[13]

After a rapid deflation, which did not, however, return prices to their previous levels, the price revolution was rekindled partly due to a continuation of the above-noted expansionary factors, but, especially after 1570, due to the rapid influx into England, and earlier in France, of Spanish silver and gold stolen from the Aztecs and Incas and subsequently mined following the Spanish conquest of the New World. Imports into Spain of gold (but mostly silver) mounted astronomically from about 1530 to 1630 and tapered off thereafter.[14] This enormous increase in the Spanish money supply poured into England and France by virtue of the large Spanish negative trade imbalances (imports greater than exports). These imbalances were themselves due to the earlier impact on prices by huge Spanish military and administrative expenses associated with war as well as the maintenance of the Spanish empire. Deficits in the foreign and public sectors in Spain thus served to funnel the specie to other countries, thereby expanding credit and the money supply there as well—hence the widespread scope of the inflation forces.

A new and vastly higher plateau of prices was thus reached by about 1650, *never to be reversed* (as indicated in figure 2.1 for England).[15] Comparative price stability, again in a long-run secular sense, for there were significant year-to-year changes, prevailed in England until about 1750. The price index then took off again, reaching an incredibly high plateau by about 1815, the end of the Napoleonic wars. This was believed initially (1750–1790) fueled by rapid expansion of bank credit, the creation of paper money, and continued international turbulence associated with the American and French Revolutions. Thereafter—in England, at least—the Napoleonic wars and large expansions of public deficits combined to drive up prices. From 1790 to 1815 prices in Great Britain are estimated to have risen by 2.8% per year—very high by historical standards. In Germany, inflation rates of over 3% per year occurred during the same interval.[16]

But the inflation quickly subsided after the end of the wars. Indeed, an almost equivalent deflation set in during the next 35 years in England, Germany, and France. In part, this deflation reflected not only the end of large military spending but also the increased capacity linked to the ongoing industrial revolution, the enormous rise in productivity, and the development of capitalism.

Once again, however, the price level never fell below its pre-Napoleonic heights reached by about 1790. All that was weeded out was the largely war-induced inflation. Indeed, depression settled on the land. Dickens vividly describes the "hungry forties" in England; all of his novels depict the misery of the working class. Karl Marx likewise depicted, along with Engels and many others, the miseries attendant on the industrial revolution—the "dark, satanic mills" and all that—while Malthus argued that the "unhappy persons [the bulk of mankind] in the great lottery of life, have drawn a blank." The business cycle began to rear its ugly head.

Deflation ended, as shown in figure 2.1, about 1850, again with many year-to-year fluctuations, only to culminate in the worldwide depression and sharp deflation from about 1873 to 1896. Prices in England, France, the United States, and Germany all decreased at rates averaging between −0.8 to −2.5% compounded annually. But even at the low point reached in 1893, the price level was above the level of a hundred years earlier in England. "Thus the peace-time inflation of the last half of the eighteenth century was a permanent one whose effects were never reversed, whereas the war-time inflation associated with the Napoleonic wars was a temporary inflation (in a secular sense) whose effects were subsequently completely reversed.[17]

To complete the story, using as a backdrop the price index shown in figure 2.1, inflation resumed after 1896 and accelerated with World War I, increasing throughout this period at compound annual rates of between 4.2% in the United States and 11% in Germany: France had an 8.2% rate and England, a 4.7% rate.[18] Sharp deflation occurred during the 1920s in a repeat performance of the post-Napoleonic war experience, and accelerated during the Great Depression, likewise a repetition of the "hungry forties" in the United Kingdom. The inflation induced by World War I was virtually wiped out by 1934, as the price level plunged almost as sharply as it had risen in England, France, and the United States. This did not happen in Germany, however, largely due to the hyperinflation of the early 1920s, which I shall discuss later in this chapter.

Inflation burgeoned again in response to World War II and its buildup in the late 1930s, but *unlike the experience of the first war, this price level movement was not even temporarily reversed, so that a permanently higher level of prices was established.*[19] This was not only true in the United Kingdom but in all Western-type democracies as well as most other countries. I shall detail the events since World War II in later chapters, with special reference to the United States. At this point, let us take stock of secular inflation through the ages and draw some conclusions and inferences from the evidence.

Given the paucity of data, it is always difficult to draw many conclusions. However, throughout history a sort of stair-step inflationary experience appears. Given any spurt in the price level, inflation systematically appears to remain at the higher level except for short-term rises, such as those associated with the Napoleonic wars and World War I. Furthermore, the stair-step effect seems to be characterized by ever-shortening (in a time sense) widths of the steps and ever-increasing heights of the steps. Thus the long-run expectation is that attacks on inflation, by whatever means, can only hope to maintain whatever level has already been reached. Certainly, the "correctives" associated with the late nineteenth century depression and the 1930s will no longer be tolerated in democratic societies. The best that can be expected therefore is some reduction in the rate of increase in the level of prices.

Most secular inflations in history have been associated with, though not necessarily caused by, a sharp and persistent rise in the money supply by various mechanisms. The increase of the money supply is now done deliberately (see chapter 4), but in the past this occurred fortuitously. At the same time, the early sixteenth-century inflation in England began well before the sharp influx of Spanish silver and gold. This inflation is often attributed to the sharp increase in population growth, with its consequent increase in demands or needs for goods and services, as well as the need to cultivate lands of lesser degree of fertility, which raised food costs rather sharply. Likewise, the inflation associated with the Black Death clearly was not strictly a monetary phenomenon. The monetary explanation of inflation only partially explains its causes.

Economies manage to survive even violent increases in the price level. The German hyperinflation, to be discussed below, is even believed to have speeded up Germany's recovery during the late 1920s. The Brazilian inflation, with inflation rates of 100% and over, was managed in such a way as not to inhibit real economic growth (see below). In a secular sense, however, the survival capabilities of economies appears to be very high. Even galloping inflation for short periods not only self-corrects but also is seen as a mere blip on the larger screen.

This is not to suggest that inflation is not a serious problem (its consequences are examined in chapter 6) but merely to note that life will go on, albeit with many inconveniences. Individuals adapt to rapidly changing circumstances in ways that perpetuate the existing system. To be sure, one can argue that the sixteenth-century price revolution hastened the demise of feudal society but that society was crumbling in any event by 1500 in western Europe. Our present society is changing as well. The advent of the secular inflation of the late 1960s and 1970s will also change the institutions, especially in the Western world. The important issue is whether these changes will improve or degrade the kind of society in which we live. Thus, despite (or perhaps because of) periodic secular inflation, the Western world has prospered, especially after the late 1770s when so-called modern economic growth began.

Yet inflation is widely regarded as a form of pestilence. Secular inflation trends over many decades do not, of course, capture the year-to-year disruption in human lives and livelihoods. While one may view with a certain, albeit queasy, equanimity the long-term secular trends, there are many, often severe, shorter-run perturbations.

Two such "events" of extreme inflation will be examined next: one, a reasonably long-term inflation covering over two decades (Brazil, 1954–1980), the other, the German hyperinflation of 1919–1923. These events will illustrate the kind of disruptions associated with high inflation rates and their aftermath.

THE BRAZILIAN EXPERIENCE

Brazil is by far the largest country in Latin America in terms of area, population, and size of annual output. Its rate of population growth and real output has likewise been among the the highest in all of Latin America since 1950. Yet Brazil has endured one of the highest rates of inflation ever experienced over such a protracted period. Indeed, Brazil "must definitely be classified as one of *the* [most] inflation-prone countries in the world."[20] Despite, or perhaps because of, the inflation and Brazil's more or less successful attempt to live with it, a brief discussion of the Brazilian experience is worthwhile. It represents a sort of halfway house between secular inflation over long time spans, as noted above, and the short-run (less than four years), violent inflationary bursts, as in the case of Germany.

At the end of World War II, the Brazilian economy, like most of the other underdeveloped economies of the world, faced bleak prospects for overall rapid growth of total output. Its economy was largely dominated by agriculture, often using primitive, low productivity techniques. Whatever economic dynamism existed was fueled mainly by exports. However, Brazil's traditional exports (coffee, cocoa, sugar, tobacco, and cotton) were believed to have but meager growth prospects. The country therefore "found itself not only among the group of nations whose exports steadily lost in the share of world trade, but also among those countries whose exports had little chance of regaining their former pre-eminence."[21]

Accordingly, in order to raise real output per head, a series of public policy strategies were attempted during the late 1940s and 1950s. Broadly speaking, these were import substitution strategies. Incentives were provided for local industries to develop domestic productive facilities to substitute for goods that were previously imported. Such facilities could be either financed from domestic or foreign sources and could be either domestically owned or owned by foreigners, preference always being given to the former, however. As with most developing economies during this period, import substitution seemed to provide the quickest way to industrialize; industrialization was in turn viewed as in some sense the key to more rapid overall economic growth.

Import substitution policies involve restrictions on those imports that can be produced domestically. Exchange controls, tariff quotas, tax preferences, and so on, are among the tools often used to reduce the economy's "dependence" on foreign sources. Brazil used the whole gamut of policies with some success.[22] Thus, real output grew at annual average rates of about 7% from 1951 through 1962, a very good overall performance by any standards.

But import substitution policies often lead to certain distortions or imbalances which, if not redressed, may slow down subsequent growth. For our purposes, it is enough to note that the rate of inflation accelerated rapidly from around 12 or 13% per year (the current rate in the United States that has aroused so much concern) to some 50% per year by 1962.[23] It is this association between the coincident rising real output and inflation rates, that led many to view the Brazilian experience as "growth by inflation." The inflation rates were fueled by rapid growth of the money supply—itself stimulated by easy credit policies, low real interest rates (i.e., actual or nominal interest rates minus the inflation rate), a large and growing public sector, and foreign balance of payments deficits.

However, after reaching a growth rate of over 10% in 1961, real output growth fell sharply in 1962, '63, and '64, averaging less than or close to the rate of population growth. In short, real output per head fell or was constant for this period. The goal of rising living standards appeared to be in jeopardy.

Inflation, growing inequalities, and other imbalances (especially the relative stagnation in agriculture, which involved the greater proportion of the population), rapid urbanization and other problems led to a series of political crises. Attempts to control inflation, for example, are always unpopular. They require, as we will examine in later chapters, such things as elimination or reduction of subsidies, always unpopular to their recipients or beneficiaries, higher interest rates, credit contractions, wage and/or price freezes, and so on. Most governments have neither the will nor the means to implement such policies. This is especially true in poor countries. Brazil was no exception.

The stagnation of the 1960s was accompanied by ever-higher inflation rates—reaching approximately 100% per year by 1964. The increasingly intolerable situation led to the overthrow of the government by a military coup in April 1964.[24]

The military government had both the will and at least some of the means to tackle the inflation problem as well as to remedy some of the imbalances that emerged in the early 1960s. A military government, after all, has certain coercive powers that are lacking under democratic institutions to resist discontent over unpopular measures. A series of measures designed to curb inflation, promote exports (not only of traditional products but some manufacturing as well), attract foreign capital, and increase investments in infrastructure (transportation, power, and other government owned enterprises, such as steel, mining, and petrochemicals) were in fact implemented. More importantly, there was a degree of perseverance in these measures that perhaps only a military regime could provide and still survive the resultant political discontent. For, indeed, stagnation of real output growth lasted until 1968, when Brazil entered "its remarkable seven-year boom."[25] Between 1962 and 1967, real output growth averaged less than 4% per year. From 1968 through 1974, this surged to over 11% and the inflation rate dropped to the 20% range. Much of the growth since 1968 was due to the impact and effectiveness of government programs as well as a fairly resilient private business sector and overall political stability.

While the evidence since 1974 shows the real growth rate declining and the inflation rate rising to the 30–40% range,[26] real output has continued to increase by over 5% per year, still a good performance record given the supply-side shocks of 1973–74 emanating from the quadrupling of oil prices and worldwide crop failures. Good luck, such as the surge of coffee prices, reasonably intelligent policies, and continuing political stability probably account for this apparent success.

We need not here enter into any detailed explanation in our cursory overview of inflationary experiences except to comment on two aspects relevant to our purpose. The first involves the "costs" paid by the Brazilian economy for its efforts to contain inflation, and the second, one of its instrumentalities, namely "indexation."

The Costs Involved

The acknowledged success especially of the 1968–74 expansion, including a sharp diversification of exports, high rates of savings and investment as well as accelerated growth and decelerated inflation, was not costless. In addition to the loss of many political freedoms, there were seriously growing economic inequalities both in terms of the personal income distribution and regional imbalances. Despite some incentives given to develop industry in the impoverished North, 80% of the industrial capacity remained in the South with barely one-third of the population. Twenty percent of the income recipients received over 65% of the national income by 1970, up from 55% ten years earlier. The poorest 40% received barely 9% of national income in 1970, down from 11.2% in 1960. While the per capita income of the poorest 40% (in U.S. dollars) rose from $84 to $90 per year between 1960 and 1970, an infinitesimal absolute rise, that of the upper 5% rose from $1,645 in 1960 to $2,940 in 1970.[27] Real wages fell during the stabilization years. Continuation of such a trend, leaving the bulk of the population at desperate levels of poverty while a small proportion reap most of the fruits of economic growth, can only lead to the miserable cycle of rising discontent, more repression, more violent forms of dissent, and so on. This is indeed the situation in much of Central and South America at present.

The "Brazilian miracle" of 1968–74 may have been bought at a cost that can't be sustained in the long run. The trade-off between economic efficiency and growth on the one hand and economic and political equality on the other hand, may have become too high. Policy modifications since 1974 have been made in recognition of this problem. It is a moot point, however, whether they are too little or too late.

Indexation

These are, of course, heady and significant problems that ought to be pursued further as they are relevant to all economies under the rubric "what price economic growth?" However, our purpose here is limited to an attempt to analyze inflation with special reference to the U.S. stagflation of the late 1960s and 1970s and to what historical experiences elsewhere suggest. In this context, one of Brazil's most innovative programs to fight inflation or at least to "learn to live with it" in 1964 was that of indexation.[28] Indexation means linking certain asset values, prices (e.g., wages), or taxes to some price index.

After many years of high inflation, the Brazilian government implemented an indexing program between 1964 and 1968. The indexation was applied to three key sectors of the Brazilian economy: the credit market, the fixed asset market, and the currency exchange market.

Over the decade of the fifties, the government had engaged in extensive deficit spending. One reason for this was the subsidization of the public utilities and transportation industries. Prices were kept artificially low and the government was forced to subsidize these industries. Likewise, due to usury laws, the government became the main source of credit for all industries, thus compounding the size of the deficit. Partially because of the deficit spending, by early 1964 the inflation rate was over 100%.

One of the distortions caused by inflation can be seen by examining the credit market. Usury laws prohibited banks from making loans in excess of 12% nominal interest rates. At the same time, interest on time deposits was limited to 6%. Once the inflation rate exceeded 12%, financial institutions had no incentive to make loans because the "real" return from the loans was negative. Likewise, when the inflation rate exceeded 6%, the saver had a strong incentive to consume out of his savings or to invest his savings in assets which provided a positive real rate of return. With the inflation rate well over 100%, the financial institutions had no incentive to make loans and the saver had no incentive to save. Thus, the supply of long-term money capital dried up. The government, to permit higher real growth, thus became the main source of credit—but only for industry, not the private sector. As a result, the housing industry, a segment of the economy whose survival is dependent upon the supply of long-term credit, nearly collapsed. To compound the problem, the government implemented rent controls. Thus, by 1964, the Brazilian economy was faced with a severe housing shortage, aggravated by very high rates of population growth.

Another distortion caused by inflation occurred in the fixed asset market. Businesses were only permitted to depreciate real production assets on a historical cost basis as opposed to a replacement cost basis. Thus, the depreciation writeoffs did not allow the firms to accumulate enough funds to replace the assets. The depreciation expenses were too low, leading to what are commonly called "illusory profits." Since businesses make decisions according to profitability, the artificially high profits did not allow investment decisions to be made in a rational manner, and higher taxes were paid on the illusory profits. Moreover, since capital is generally distributed according to profitability, there was a distortion in its distribution.

Still another distortion caused by the inflation occurred in the import-export market. Since the country only devalued its currency twice a year, the demand for imports increased because import prices were not increasing by as much as domestic prices. At the same time, Brazil's exports became less competitive on the world market because their prices were higher. As a result, Brazil's balance of payments deficits soared.

By implementing the indexing program, the Brazilian authorities had decided to live with inflation. The program outlined three areas which were to be indexed. The first area concerned the indexing of all fixed industrial assets. The government permitted depreciation to be charged on the assets' revalued base. This program was aimed at eliminating illusory profits, thus enhancing the firm's ability to make rational decisions. The second area of the program concerned the credit market. To finance its large deficit spending, the government authorized the issuing of a series of government bonds referred to as "Readjustable National Treasury Obligations." These bonds were primarily of one to two years in maturity. The principal value of these bonds were adjusted upward monthly according to a three-month moving average of the *past* inflation rate, a practice commonly called post indexing. In addition, the government created the National Housing Bank. Bonds issued by this bank to finance loans were indexed. Likewise, the mortgage loans issued by the bank were indexed. The third area of the program was aimed at encouraging exports and attracting foreign capital. The government created the "crawling peg" exchange rate. This provided for the devaluation of the currency[29] several times during the year. Although the devaluation was not directly related to the inflation rate, as a general rule the government devalued the currency as the rate of inflation increased.

What were the results of the indexing program? First, the partial resolution of the illusory profits problem permitted firms to make more rational investment decisions. As a result of the government issuing indexed bonds and indexing tax liabilities (which speeded up tax collections), the budget deficit as a percentage of GDP[30] decreased from over 4% in 1964 to 0.17% in 1972. With the formation of the National Housing Bank, the savings rate increased tremendously, and the severe housing shortage of the early sixties was reduced. Yet another benefit of the program was the rapid growth in exports. Moreover, with the devaluation of the currency, the amount of foreign capital inflow grew from $0.697 billion between 1965 and 1969 to over $4.7 billion by 1973. One problem caused by the substantial inflow was that more capital has been attracted than can be productively absorbed, thus leading to very high foreign indebtedness without a corresponding increase in productive capacity.

Some of the distortion problems in the Brazilian economy have been solved. By indexing fixed assets, the firms have a better statement of their true profits. Likewise, by indexing credit instruments, the real rate of interest is known: thus, creditors and debtors know their real returns. Finally, by pegging the exchange rate to the inflation rate, the export market has boomed and foreign capital has been attracted.

But wage rates were never indexed, although many wages were directly or indirectly set by guidelines from the government that took account of inflation, actual or anticipated. As noted above, not only did this worsen the overall income distribution but inflation surged again after 1974.

Recent analyses suggest that indexing did permit mobilization of larger savings in the form of government and housing bonds and savings accounts. However, direct financing of private business through stock or bond sales was inhibited, since these were not indexed. Private businesses were therefore required to have further recourse, for their financial needs, to government credit and foreign loans. The government and many foreign lending agencies provided these. The government financed its loans by creating more credit which aggravated inflation. Foreign loans were forthcoming partly because the prospects of such a large economy with abundant resources seemed propitious and partly to reinforce the viability of enterprises previously supported.

But this process becomes self-reinforcing, perpetuates inflation and ever-increasing dependence on the public sector for the financing of various enterprises. As has been said, "Brazil's index-linking system has . . . led to more than economic planners bargained for . . . and when the rate of inflation suddenly jumped upward, index-linking became a nuisance."[31] This system worked for a while during the 1960s and early 1970s by encouraging thrift, but it has created a "barely controlled . . . inflationary momentum."[32]

The side effects of indexation now appear to have outweighed their probable positive benefits in the "miracle" period 1968–74. Indeed the inflation rate was estimated at 113% in 1980,[33] and severe modifications of the past indexing schemes are being put in place.

Implications of the Brazilian Experience

Clearly, very high rates of inflation are compatible either with high rates of real economic growth or with sluggish growth and high unemployment. The former typified Brazil in the 1950s, the latter, the 1960s. The 1970s in Brazil presents a much more mixed picture, but the economy appears to have worsened in recent years.

Efforts to control excessive and/or rising inflation rates led to the downfall of political liberalism, however imperfect, in Brazil. The military has been in control since 1964. The role of the government in the economy increased sharply—in part by eliminating some previous interventions (e.g., usury laws), but mostly by increasing the ability of the government to shape resource allocation and, to a lesser extent, overall growth. The successes of public policies during the late 1960s and early 1970s cannot be attributed to a "market-oriented" solution. Direct and substantial public intervention partly explain the limited successes achieved.

But such interventions led to rising regional and personal inequalities that by the mid-1970s were becoming more and more disfunctional as inflation accelerated and real growth sputtered.

The road to price stability or even steady state inflation at or below double-digit levels, is seemingly long and rocky.

THE GERMAN HYPERINFLATION, 1919–1923

The Brazilian inflation experience has been one of high and sharply fluctuating prices over a long period of time. The German post–World War I inflation was unique. At no time in history has an economy experienced such a dramatic rise in prices over such a short period of time as the German economy did between 1919–1923. In 1919, the German wholesale price index stood at 8.03 (1913 = 1); in just four years, the wholesale price index had risen to the astounding figure of 1,200,400,000,000.00.[34] "In the fall of 1923 even a box of matches sold for more marks than were in existence in pre-war Germany."[35] There is much controversy over what actually caused the great inflation, but there is no doubt that the dramatic increase in the money supply helped fuel the inflation spiral. In December 1919, the money supply (in millions) stood at 50,065 marks. Four years later, in December 1923, the issue of marks stood at 496,585,345,900.00.[36] At the climax of the inflation spiral, people were required to carry boxes full of paper money in order to make small purchases. Furthermore, at the end, the mark ceased to function as money. Only "real" goods had value.

> A story is told of two women carrying to the bank a laundry basket filled to the brim with banknotes. Seeing a crowd round a shop window, they put down their basket for a moment to see if there was anything that they could buy. When they turned around a few minutes later, they found the money still there untouched. But the basket was gone.[37]

In November 1923, with the adoption of a new medium of exchange, the Rentenmark, the great inflation ended. The old mark had ceased to satisfy the functions of money—namely, a medium of exchange, a store of value, and a standard of deferred payments.

To explain the dramatic episode, we begin with the First World War. With the onset of World War I, the German government decided that instead of financing the war through higher taxes, it would sell treasury bonds. The idea was that the German citizens should not have to pay for the war and that the enemy would pay after victory was achieved. The treasury bonds issued were not only issued to finance the war, they were also issued to serve as backing for the currency. Prior to the war, Germany's monetary system was based on the Bank Law of 1875. This law required that the currency in circulation be backed one-third by gold and two-thirds by commercial bills—that is, bills guaranteed "by persons of proven solvency."[38] With the tremendous amount of war financing required, the treasury bonds also were allowed to serve as backing for the currency, thus paving the way for a sharp increase in the money supply. Moreover, the German government recalled all gold coins in circulation. By doing this, for every 20 gold marks brought in, the Reichsbank, Germany's central bank, could issue 60 paper marks.

In 1918, at the end of the war, the price level had only doubled, although the money supply had risen from 5,862 million marks to 32,937 million marks and the amount of floating debt had climbed from 5,158 million marks to 105,304 million marks.[39] With the large amount of public debt in the hands of the public—which could be converted to liquidity—along with a severe shortage of goods, there was an enormous amount of inflationary pressure put on the economy. To compound the problem, the productive capacity of the economy had decreased due to the war. Though extensive devastation and physical destruction did not occur, yet the shortage of materials during the war and the urgency of obtaining immediate yields led to an inability to repair and maintain much of the capital assets. An "extreme deterioration in equipment of all types"[40] occurred. The output per man had been reduced by more than two-thirds in 1919 compared with the prewar level. Moreover, industrial production had been geared toward the production of war goods. The productivity of agricultural land was also diminished by one-third.[41] To complicate matters, the signing of the Versailles Treaty on 28 June 1919, forced Germany to cede 13% of her prewar territory, including the valuable districts of Upper Silesia and Alsace-Lorraine, which contained one-third of Germany's coal production; 40% of her blast furnaces; and 10% of her iron and steel foundries.[42]

The decline in productive capacity, along with the loss of these territories, caused chronic shortages and reduced Germany's exporting ability. Since Germany needed to import vast amounts of goods in order to replace her existing and deteriorated capital stock, exports were needed to avoid serious balance of payments deficits. With the loss of Upper

Silesia and Alsace-Lorraine, Germany's ability to produce and export was greatly diminished. Germany was forced to borrow from abroad to finance the growing trade deficit. However, as world banks began to speculate that Germany would not be able to repay these loans, the exchange rate began to fall; the price of imported goods rose. Since the demand for foreign capital goods was relatively insensitive to prices, the needed equipment was imported at higher and higher prices, thus adding fuel to the inflation spiral—not unlike our current oil import situation.

Other countries, such as England and the United States, urged Germany to take steps to balance the government's budget. These countries had experienced inflation during the war, and afterwards sought to balance their budgets and implement strict credit policies, thereby reducing total spending and the rate of inflation. But Germany was in the process of rebuilding her economy, and this required large amounts of imports, thus leading to a large increase in government outlays. Germany had also incurred extremely large postwar expenses, such as military demobilization and veteran's benefits. Germany therefore continued to run a balance of payments and public sector deficit. To magnify the deficit problem, with the loss of the two districts mentioned above, Germany's tax base had been severely eroded. As inflation increased, and by the time the government received tax payments, the purchasing power of the money had been severely reduced.[43]

Many experts thought that with increased tax revenues, along with rebuilding the capital stock, inflation would be brought under control, and the economy could even prosper.

But the economic bubble quickly broke. Article 231 of the Versailles Treaty required Germany to compensate the allies for damages resulting from the war, thereby acknowledging its guilt for the war. On 5 May 1921, the Reparation Committee made its demands on the German government. The committee called for 132 milliard (thousand millions) gold marks to be paid in annual installments of 2 milliard marks, plus 26% of the value of Germany's exports.[44] One-half of the first installment was due in August. At first, Germany refused to meet these demands, but with the threat of allied occupation, the German government accepted these terms. As Graham states, "The allies began by demanding the impossible and they capriciously imposed sanctions when the impossible was not performed."[45] Upon payment of the first installment, the supply of marks flooded the world market, thus leading to a decline in the exchange value of the mark. To compound the problem, there was a great deal of speculation among foreigners and German citizens. The Germans were rapidly losing faith in the mark, so they began to convert marks into foreign currency, further flooding the market and leading to an even greater decline in the exchange rate.

As the decline in the mark was translated into higher and higher prices, the government continued to issue treasury bonds to cover its increasing foreign payments deficit. The savings rate of the economy had dropped to a negative level as the public's demand for treasury bonds vanished. The Reichsbank (central bank) was forced to purchase the debt and monetize the debt. With the decline in the savings rate, the commercial banks were being starved for deposits. This caused a severe shortage of credit.

In the summer of 1922, the government urged the adoption once again of the commercial bill as a means of backing the currency. By doing so, the commercial banks would have a source of funds available for credit. However, this allowed the commercial banks to contribute to the further expansion of the money supply. The disastrous consequence of the adoption of the commercial bill is illustrated by Graham's statement, "The Reichsbank could not refuse to discount Treasury bills but the policy on commercial bills was a gratuitous mortification of an already fatal wound."[46] The loans issued by the commercial banks had an interest rate pegged at 5%. This rate was allowed to rise and reached its height of 900% in September of 1923.[47] But, considering the rise in prices, this was still a negative real rate of interest—shades of Brazil.

At the beginning of 1922, the German government notified the Reparation Committee that it could not meet the next reparation installment. The Morgan Committee was established to investigate the feasibility of arranging a foreign loan so that Germany could finance this installment. The French government refused such an idea. They insisted that Germany pay for its war crimes. With this news, the exchange rate plunged.

In the fateful year of 1923, the inflation rate was completely out of control. And the government was on the brink of bankruptcy. At the height of the hyperinflation (summer of 1923), government revenues were only 3% of its total expenditures. It financed the remaining 97% by printing money. As Guttman states, "thousands of printing presses disgorged mountains of pieces of paper called 'money,' which were rushed . . . to desperately waiting crowds, hoping to get the stuff in time to buy the necessities of life before inflation had made it worthless."[48] Businesses refused to sell goods because to replenish existing stock would result in huge losses. Likewise, the agricultural sector, despite a bumper harvest, refused to sell farm products because of the worthless mark, thus resulting in widespread starvation. The Germany economy was no longer competitive on the world markets. Even with the falling exchange rate, it could sell its products only by dumping them on the world market. As the economy began to grind to a halt, the final blow was delivered by the French government. Dissatisfied with reparation payments in kind that were not delivered, France occupied the main industrial area of Germany, the Ruhr. In retaliation, the German government ordered work stoppages in this area so that the French could not benefit from the productive capacity of this area. By the end of the summer, the economy had virtually collapsed. Unemployment rose from one percent in 1922 to over 23% in November of 1923.[49] The mark no longer functioned as a medium of exchange.

On 15 November 1923, a miracle occurred. The great inflation came to an end! The government took action to stabilize the economy by issuing a new currency, the so-called Rentenmark. Along with the new currency came strict credit controls designed to limit the expansion of the money supply and increase its acceptability. The Rentenmark served as the new medium of exchange only because the people wanted so desperately for it to succeed.

How does one explain this apparent miracle? From the depths of despair, the Germany economy rebounded after 1923 and achieved real growth rates larger than England, one of the victors of the war and the country that did not endure such a vicious hyperinflation. Indeed, it has been argued that the great inflation allowed the German economy to recover much faster than it would have had the inflation not occurred. While other countries were undertaking deflationary programs and experiencing longish periods of stagnation (only the United States enjoyed the "roaring twenties"), the German economy prospered after 1923. Moreover, as a result of these deflationary programs in England, investment dropped sharply, thus eroding the capital stock. In the German case, with rising prices and falling real wages, businesses were given the incentive to invest, thus rebuilding the war-devastated capital stock with more recent technology after the advent of the Rentenmark and price stability. If a deflationary program had been implemented, the economy might have stagnated longer, creating the potential for a political uprising.[50] It can also be argued that the inflationary period resulted in serious distortions and inequality and that if continued longer, as in Brazil, would have been economically counterproductive. But the fact remains that Germany recovered much faster from the war damage than would have been possible under a contradictory, deflation program.

IMPLICATIONS

There is no completely satisfactory explanation of the Rentenmark miracle that turned the short-run inflationary devastation into a positive resumption of real economic growth faster than that of the allies. Perhaps it is true that in Germany, when the Rentenmark was devised and issued, "it was an event that created faith,"[51] optimism, and hope. Such is the fragility and tenuous psychological basis of economic stability. Life does go on even under the most trying circumstances. Perhaps it is also true that such cataclysmic experiences jolt societies out of certain predetermined ruts, that great challenges elicit great responses. President Roosevelt's assertion in the depths of the Great Depression that we have "nothing to fear but fear itself" and his programs for reform obviously restored generalized hope for better days in much the same way that the announcement of currency reform in November 1923 did in Germany.

There is, of course, no certainty that appropriate responses will be forthcoming. But in our brief review of past inflations it is evident that these economies survived and subsequently prospered by variously learning to live with inflation through innovative measures (Brazilian indexation, currency, and institutional reform in Germany), good luck, an overall belief that the economic world could and would endure (albeit in different form), and/or the high degree of adaptability of the people enduring such disruptions.

Other countries in the past have experienced relatively short hyperinflations analogous to that of Germany. Most of these were associated with war and its aftermath. For example, Austria suffered an 11-month hyperinflation (October 1921 to August 1922) with average *monthly* price increases of 47%; Greece (November 1943 to November 1944) had average monthly price increases of 365%; Hungary experienced two hyperinflations (March 1923 to February 1924 and August 1945 to July 1946) with monthly inflation rates of 46% and 19,800% (!), respectively; Poland (January 1923 to January 1924) had an average monthly price index increase of 81%.[52]

More recently, triple-digit (i.e., over 100% per *year*) inflation has beset several countries. Between 1970 and 1978 prices are estimated to have risen at an *annual* rate of 243% in Chile and 120% in Argentina.[53] During 1979 and 1980, inflation rates over or close to 100% per year were recorded in Brazil, Israel, and Zaire.

These are extreme cases. Yet inflation rates in almost every country have increased sharply during the 1970s as compared with the 1960s.[54]

The challenge of high and variable rates of inflation, as presently besets most countries of the world, will, as in the past, evoke responses of one kind or another. Such inflation—whether secular, high, and/or variable—does indeed create large economic and social inequities and does affect overall growth of living standards. The historical record suggests that even hyperinflation may be therapeutic economically, although not politically.[55] The responses to high inflation are often of the extreme "right wing" variety: austerity imposed by an authoritarian regime, as is currently the vogue in much of Latin America. Price, wage, and import controls on the one hand or a "market solution" on the other hand, regardless of short-run consequences, are, in varying degrees, being experimented with everywhere. Both solutions involve an increasingly activist role by governments—either in specific changes of the rules of the economic game via detailed intervention, subsidy, indexation, and the like (as in Brazil), or in generalized overall policies designed to restrict credit, balance the budget and raise (or lower) some taxes (as in Mrs. Thatcher's England). None are assured of success. None reckon the economic and social costs. Is a one percent reduction in the inflation rate worth an estimated 10 percent reduction in real output and its associated rise in unemployment? What are the trade-offs, economically and politically, of alternative approaches to the inflation problem? Is it really a serious problem?

To attempt answers to these questions, it is necessary to examine the *causes* of inflation and the nature of the trade-offs. There are obviously many causal factors at work and different kinds of trade-offs that affect various social groups in different ways. The following chapters seek to sort out the causes and consequences of the kind of inflation currently besetting the U.S. economy in particular.

3 Causes of Inflation

INTRODUCTION

Most continuing inflations are initiated and sustained by an excess of spending in the economy as a whole. That is, when people, groups, businesses, government, and foreigners all together "demand" or try to spend more than the economy can produce at full employment, prices in general will be bid up. Until the excess demand for goods and services is reduced and/or the capacity of the economy to produce is expanded, the price level will continue to rise.

In simplified form, figure 3.1 indicates what is widely believed to be the relationship of total spending to total real output (deflated GNP) and "capacity."

The curve S_1S_1 represents the assumed relationship between an increase in output and the level of prices, defined as the aggregate supply curve. That is, for levels of real output or production below X_1, the economy has plenty of excess capacity, if capacity is at X_C. This means that there are "idle men and machines." Hence, output can be increased without a significant increase in wage rates or other production costs. Unit costs of production with a high degree of slack would not be expected to rise as unutilized capacity and unemployed labor are brought into production. Indeed, if some business costs vary less than in proportion to volume of production, then for those sectors average costs of production should decline even with constant wage rates. Thus, increases in spending, represented by shifts in the DD curve that "call forth" increased production, should not lead to a large (if any) increase in the general price level—at least up to some point such as X_1.

In short, expansions of production induced by increased total spending (shifts in DD) are compatible with price level stability or only minor increases in some overall index, so long as "considerable" excess capacity exists in the economy, as was the case during the 1930s. To be sure, some prices and costs might rise as output expands because of particular bottlenecks in some industries. All industries will not, of course, have the

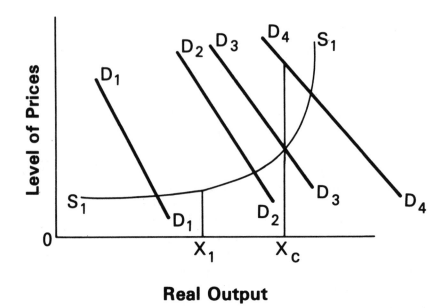

Real Output

Fig. 3.1

same degree of excess capacity. Thus, whether the price level rises somewhat or remains relatively stable will depend upon the pattern, the industrial distribution, of the overall increase in spending. If much of the
increased spending (or demand) is directed to industries or takes place
in regions of the country with less slack than for the nation as a whole,
there will be a greater inflationary impact (and vice versa). But, given a
high degree of overall slack, especially large amounts of labor unemployment for output levels below X_C (and certainly below X_1), the *overall*
effect on the price index will generally be small.

Thus, although *real* output increased by over 44% from the depths of
the Great Depression in 1933 through 1937, the consumer price index
rose by less than 11% over the four-year period, as did the implicit GNP
price deflator. In short, for situations of considerable slack in the economy, increases in production associated with rising total spending are
compatible with relatively mild increases in prices.

However, as total spending (often referred to as "nominal" GNP,
which is total output of final goods and services measured in current
rather than base period prices) rises beyond X_1 (e.g., D_1D_1 shifts to
D_2D_2), the upward pressure on the price level mounts, partly because

more bottlenecks of one sort and another are encountered, or because overtime pay for particular grades of labor in relatively short supply is necessitated. In addition, as business firms come to anticipate higher levels of demand, as well as experiencing somewhat higher costs, the price level will rise faster. Thus, an increase in nominal GNP will come to be divided into an increasingly higher proportion of price rise compared to real output increase. For example, between 1933 and 1937, when nominal GNP increased by approximately 55%, most of the increase ($80\% = \frac{44\%}{55\%}$) represented real output. The economy was operating well below X_1. However, in the recovery from the 1974–75 recession, *nominal* GNP rose from 1975 to 1978 by 39%, whereas real GNP rose by only 16%. In short, only about 40% of the rise in nominal GNP represented a real output increase. The reason usually given is that there was considerably less slack or excess capacity in the U.S. economy in 1974 than in 1933.[1]

The closer the economy gets to capacity GNP (X_C), the worse becomes the trade-off between real output increases and price level increases, as indicated in figure 3.1. As aggregate demand or total spending shifts to the right (to D_3D_3 and D_4D_4), the aggregate supply curve (S_1S_1) gets steeper.

How is it possible to increase real output beyond the capacity of the system? The notion of capacity is elastic. It presupposes some full-employment unemployment level, say 4–6%. Employment, and hence output, can, however, increase even beyond this. During World War II, total spending associated with defense and growing manpower shortages associated with the draft, lured many people into the labor force who would not normally be there. Higher wage rates and the desire to contribute something tangible to the war effort caused this. Thus unemployment rates fell below 2% in 1943, 1944, and 1945, far below the then full-employment unemployment rate.

Not only is the concept of capacity elastic in this sense (and hence the line drawn vertically from X_C in figure 3.1 should really be drawn as a relatively thick band), but capacity, the ability to produce goods and services, regularly expands with the growth of the labor force and the other productive assets of the nation, such as the capital stock and technical knowledge. In addition, the quality of the labor force and capital stock improves over time associated with technological change, improved skills, technical, manual and managerial, resulting in a rightward shift in the aggregate supply curve.

This means that not only does the resource base of the economy expand, but the output per unit of resource input does likewise over time. For short-run periods, such expansion of capacity is not very large. Until recently, it was put at about 4 to $4\frac{1}{2}$% per year for the postwar U.S. economy—a combination of a 2 to 3% increase in the labor force and a $1\frac{1}{2}$ to 2% increase in total real output per year *on the average*. More recently, with the sharp decrease in productivity and some slowing down of labor force growth, the capacity of the economy is believed to be increasing at closer to 2% than 4%.

In any event, the behavior of prices illustrated in figure 3.1 is broadly descriptive of what may be viewed as excess demand inflation—namely, a situation in which DD keeps shifting to the right against an aggregate supply curve that rises ever more steeply as the degree of actual excess capacity decreases. This shift is modified by annual increases in capacity (rightward shifts in aggregate supply) that, at least over the last decade in the United States, likewise has diminished.

The question to be raised now is, why does total spending (DD) continue to increase against a more slowly increasing capacity to produce? To answer this we need to examine the determinants of the spending categories that economists have found useful to distinguish—namely, personal consumption expenditures (C), gross private domestic investment (I), government GNP purchases (G), and net foreign investment (exports less imports or $X - M$).

The most important determinants of consumption expenditures are the levels of personal disposable income and personal wealth. The former includes household income from all sources (wages, interest, dividends, etc., less taxes), while the latter includes money (cash on hand plus demand and savings deposits), stocks, bonds, and physical assets such as automobiles, houses, clothing, furniture, and so on. Empirical research shows that aggregate consumption varies directly with the level of income and the level of real wealth. That is, the higher household disposable income and the value of the aggregate of monetary and nonmonetary assets, the greater is aggregate consumption. Thus, anything affecting these determinants of spending will influence the level of consumption expenditures in the same direction. A reduction in personal income taxes will raise disposable household income and hence increase consumption. A rise in the price level will lower the purchasing power of money balances (i.e., real balances) but will often raise the money value of houses and other physical assets. The effect on stock and bond values, however, depends on what the rise in the price level does to nominal and real interest rates and other influences. The net impact of a rise in the price level on personal consumption expenditures is therefore difficult to predict. By lowering the real value of money balances, people may reduce consumption to reestablish such balances. However, if the value of other assets is raised by the price increase, much or all of this impact may be blunted. Indeed, as we will see later, if further price rises are anticipated, consumption spending may rise as people seek to purchase certain durable items prior to any more price increases.

Nevertheless, there is a close connection between consumption spending and disposable personal income. This means that federal government policy can more or less directly affect aggregate consumption by changing income tax rates—raising them to reduce consumption and lowering them to stimulate consumption—or by changing the volume of transfer payments (i.e., welfare payments, unemployment compensation, etc.). Such deliberate tax rate and transfer payment changes[2] are referred to as *fiscal policy*.

Business investment expenditures, or expenditures on newly produced plant, machinery, and equipment are determined by their expected profitability compared with the rate of interest. If the expected rate of return of a new asset exceeds the rate of interest, the new asset will in general be produced, thereby adding to total expenditure. By changing business tax rates and by altering the rate of interest through deliberate money supply management—*monetary policy*—the volume of new investment can be influenced by the administration, Congress, or Federal Reserve System (the Central Bank).

The level of federal government expenditures largely depends on past and present policies with respect to various sectors of the economy (e.g., defense, natural resources, welfare, agriculture, energy, etc.). To stimulate total spending, the federal government can directly increase its purchases from the private sector. These purchases clearly raise aggregate spending directly by the amount of the increase, but they also have further impact on private spending. The rise in government spending increases incomes in the private sector and this will induce more private consumption and perhaps investments—the so-called multiplier effect. Opposite reactions occur when government spending is reduced.

Exports minus imports are less directly affected by government policy except through changes in tariffs, quotas, and the like. American exports depend largely on the economic health of foreign economies, the value of the dollar vis-à-vis other currencies, trade policies, and so on—similarly with imports.

The foregoing brief sketch of the determinants of total spending in the economy as a whole indicates certain key variables that can be manipulated by public policy (such as tax rates, government spending on goods and services or transfer payments, and the money supply). The standard Keynesian textbook analysis proposes that if total spending in the economy (aggregate demand) is too low to generate full employment, the public policy response *should be* some combination of a reduction in the rate of taxation, an increase in the level of government spending and an increase in the money supply at a faster rate. On the other hand, if aggregate demand is too high and generates inflationary pressures, the policy responses *should be* the opposite of the above.

The name of the policy game, more or less actively pursued in Western, democratic, largely market-oriented economies ever since World War II, has been to try to control the level of aggregate spending to ensure relatively full employment (and certainly prevent another recession of the magnitude of 1929–33) and relatively stable prices. In general, the aim was to ensure that, once full employment was reached, total spending should be allowed to increase at rates no faster than the expanding capacity of the economy to produce.

However, aggregate demand would be expected to grow (i.e., DD would shift to the right), even without expansionist government policies. This tendency is due to continued growth in population, which increases demands for more goods and services. Even with a stationary population, however, demands for more or different goods can be expected to emerge in our consumer-oriented society. Business will respond to these demands by making new investments or creating new demands as technology develops or as styles and tastes change. Thus, new incomes are generated, most of which will be spent in one way or another. Similarly, foreign demands for U.S. products increase over time and generate incomes with similar impacts on spending. In short, aggregate demand keeps increasing. The problem for inflation control is to ensure that the rate of expansion of spending does not exceed the growing capacity of the economy to produce.

The capacity of the economy itself increases over time (i.e., the aggregate supply curve shifts to the right in figure 3.1) due to the increase in the labor force (itself due to population growth), the increase of the nation's capital stock (due to net investment per year), and the increase in productivity (output per man) due to technological change and improvements in labor and management skills and education.

The economy, then, to ensure reasonable price stability and reasonably full employment, must try to limit the growth rate of total spending to that of the growth of capacity. This often requires the conscious use of monetary and fiscal policies to restrain or to stimulate aggregate spending. In addition, however, policies can be directed toward increasing the growth of capacity of the system—so-called supply-side economics. In the long-run fight against inflation, this, combined with sensible demand management could be decisive. For the moment, however, we will concentrate on the demand side.

To a large degree, these "demand management" activities on the part of the central government worked well in most democracies from the end of World War II until at least the mid-1960s. At that time, largely due to excessive demand stimulus in the United States associated with the Indochina War, the increasing costs of President Johnson's Great Society programs, and an unwillingness to raise taxes accordingly or pursue enough monetary restraint, the rate of increase of the CPI shot up from 1.7% in 1965 to 5.9% by 1970 (see table 3.1). Although it receded in 1971–72, possibly aided by price controls, by 1974 it reached 11%. The recession of 1974–75 reduced the rate of increase to 5.8% in 1976, but the rate has risen steadily since then and during the first quarter of 1980 was estimated at an annual rate in the 15–18% range—an unprecedented rate of inflation for the U.S. economy, either in peace or war.

The U.S. inflation experience since 1968 has indeed been dismal. But what seems equally disturbing is that the rate of increase in the CPI remains very high (by past standards), even when the unemployment rate, indicative of large amounts of excess capacity in the economy, is also very high. Thus, as table 3.2 indicates, an inflation rate over 9% was consistent with an unemployment rate of 8.5% in 1975. To be sure, following the end of the recession in 1975, the inflation rate fell, indicating a somewhat lagging adjustment between price increases and unemployment. But even the drop in the inflation rate to 5.8% in 1976 indicates an exceptionally high rate compared with the experience from 1950 through 1968.

It appears therefore that the U.S. economy during the late 1960s and all of the 1970s suffered a sharp upward shift in what has been called the built-in or basic inflation rate. This means that for degrees of excess capacity which in the past were associated with comparative price stability, now comparable degrees of slack are compatible with significantly higher rates of inflation. Indeed if we add the inflation and unemployment rates to get what Arthur Okun has dubbed the "discomfort index," we note from table 3.2 (last column) a significant upward trend, especial-

TABLE 3.1

Price Behavior in the U.S. Economy
Year-to-Year Percentage Changes
1948–1979

Year	Consumer Price Index	Producer Price Index	GNP_Deflator
1948	7.8	8.0	6.9
1949	−1.0	−2.9	−1.0
1950	1.0	1.8	2.0
1951	7.9	9.5	6.8
1952	2.2	−0.6	1.3
1953	0.8	−1.0	1.5
1954	0.5	0.2	1.4
1955	−0.4	0.2	2.2
1956	1.5	2.8	3.2
1957	3.6	3.6	3.4
1958	2.7	2.3	1.6
1959	0.8	−0.2	2.2
1960	1.6	0.8	1.7
1961	1.0	0	0.9
1962	1.1	0.3	1.8
1963	1.2	−0.3	1.5
1964	1.3	0.4	1.6
1965	1.7	1.7	2.2
1966	2.9	3.2	3.3
1967	2.9	1.2	2.9
1968	4.2	2.9	4.5
1969	5.4	3.6	5.0
1970	5.9	3.5	5.4
1971	4.3	3.1	5.1
1972	3.3	3.1	4.1
1973	6.2	9.1	5.8
1974	11.0	15.3	9.7
1975	9.1	10.8	9.6
1976	5.8	4.2	5.2
1977	6.5	6.0	6.0
1978	7.7	7.8	7.3
1979	11.3	10.9	8.8

Source: *Annual Report of the Council of Economic Advisers*, Washington, D.C.,
1980.

TABLE 3.2

The Relationship between Unemployment and Inflation

Year	Unemployment Rate (percent)	Five Year Average	Percent Change of Consumer Price Index from Previous Year	Five Year Average	Five Year Average of the Sums
1950	5.3		+ 0.9		6.2
1951	3.3		+ 8.0		11.3
1952	3.0	4.0	+ 2.2	2.5	5.2	6.5
1953	2.9		+ 0.8		3.7
1954	5.5		+ 0.4		5.9
1955	4.4		− 0.3		4.1
1956	4.1		+ 1.5		5.6
1957	4.3	5.0	+ 3.5	1.7	7.8	6.8
1958	6.8		+ 2.8		9.6
1959	5.5		+ 1.2		6.7
1960	5.5		+ 1.6		7.1
1961	6.7		+ 1.1		7.8
1962	5.5	5.7	+ 1.2	1.3	6.7	7.0
1963	5.7		+ 1.2		6.9
1964	5.2		+ 1.3		6.5
1965	4.5		+ 1.7		6.2
1966	3.8		+ 3.0		6.8
1967	3.8	3.8	+ 2.8	3.4	6.6	7.2
1968	3.6		+ 3.9		7.5
1969	3.5		+ 5.4		8.9
1970	4.9		+ 5.9		10.8
1971	5.9		+ 4.3		10.2
1972	5.6	5.4	+ 3.3	6.1	8.9	11.5
1973	4.9		+ 6.2		11.1
1974	5.6		+10.9		16.5
1975	8.5		+ 9.1		17.6
1976	7.7		+ 5.8		12.3
1977	7.0	7.0	+ 6.5	7.8	13.5	14.8
1978	6.0		+ 7.7		13.3
1979	5.8		+ 9.9		15.7

Source: Annual Report of the Council of Economic Advisers, U.S. Government Printing Office, Washington, D.C., various years; and Economic Indicators, U.S. Government Printing Office, Washington, D.C., various months.

ly since 1969. In fact, taking five-year averages from 1950 through 1979, the trend has been upward—but a dramatic increase has occurred since the five-year period from 1965 through 1969. Thus, for the last five years of the 1970s, rates of inflation exceeding 7% have been compatible with rates of unemployment of about 7%.

It is also worth noting that in no recession since 1950 has the CPI (or the GNP deflator) fallen. (See table 3.1). Its rate of increase has slowed but only after somewhat of a lag. This is contrary to the experience of recessions prior to World War II. It is therefore evident that high and rising rates of inflation have increasingly become consistent with high and even rising rates of unemployment.

The implications of our experience since the mid-1960s is that both inflation and unemployment must have causes in addition to an excess or deficiency of aggregate spending relative to the capacity of the economy to produce. This possibility came as a distinct shock to many economists whose basic model of the economy implied that serious inflation was caused solely by an excess of spending relative to capacity, while serious unemployment was caused solely by a deficiency of spending. For, if that were true, it would be logically impossible to have *both* high and rising prices and unemployment at the same time. But the recent economic performance indicates that this is indeed the case. The simplistic, unicausal explanation implicit in the earlier Keynesian formulations can no longer be accepted. Nor can the earlier finding of a stable trade-off between inflation and unemployment, often referred to as the Phillips curve, be accepted.

A DIGRESSION ON THE PHILLIPS CURVE

The Phillips curve was first developed from a set of observations by A. W. Phillips in 1958 that related wage rate changes to the unemployment rate over a long period of time in the United Kingdom. In the United States this was quickly translated into the inverse relationship between the rate of inflation and the rate of unemployment, changes in the price level being related to changes in wage rates. The higher the inflation rate (percentage change of the CPI or other price index), the lower the unemployment rate and vice versa. Initially, this was viewed as a reasonably stable trade-off. Thus, if the sum of these two rates was believed to be reasonably stable or followed a specific inverse relationship (i.e., the discomfort index noted above), policymakers could then opt for a particular but constrained combination of overall **unemploy-ment** and inflation by monetary and fiscal policies.[3] Data on the actual rates of unemployment and inflation in the United States from 1962 to 1972 broadly appeared to validate a relatively stable trade-off, though not a linear relationship.[4]

However, since the early 1970s, the relationship has become much less stable, even nonexistent. Higher and higher unemployment rates are consistent with any given rate of inflation. The Phillips curve has shifted outward very rapidly in the last decade. Indeed, since the unemployment and inflation rates often change in the same direction, it is not self-evident that a trade-off even exists.

The Phillips curve, however, is partially rescued by viewing the actual inflation rate as determined by both the *expected* inflation rate and the level of unemployment relative to the full-employment unemployment rate. The higher the expected rate of inflation, the higher the actual rate for any given unemployment rate. Since the experience of inflation during the 1970s perpetuates the expectation of its continuance, the Phillips curve has constantly shifted outward. That is, the trade-off, if it exists, has become worse in the sense that to reduce the rate of inflation appears to require ever greater amounts of unemployment and vice versa (see table 3.2).

EXPLAINING THE INEXPLICABLE

To return to the earlier theme, how can prices rise even in an economy with considerable slack or excess capacity in the form of idle men and machines? A corollary question is, why do prices not fall or the rate of increase in prices not fall very much during recent recessions as they did prior to World War II?

The phenomenon being examined involves attempts to explain why the unemployment rate appears to have shifted upward sharply during the 1970s as compared with the previous 20 years. That is, from 1950 through 1969 the average annual unemployment rate was 4.6%. From 1970 through 1979 the rate averaged 6.2%, an increase of about one-third. The puzzle is that during the 1970s, inflation rates also accelerated, thereby indicating an excess demand which, according to the excess demand explanation of inflation, should have led to *decreased* unemployment rates. In fact, inflation rates rose from an average annual rate of 2.2% (1950 through 1969) to an annual average rate of almost 7% during the 1970s (see table 3.2). Why?

Data Problems

The CPI as an indicator of inflation may overstate its rate of increase. The CPI is only one of several overall price indexes regularly published. It is calculated on a different basis from some other indexes, notably the GNP deflator. In the context of rising inflation rates over the last five years, the CPI gives distinctly higher rates than the GNP deflator or even the personal consumption expenditure component of the GNP deflator. Table 3.1 indicates that during 1979, the CPI grew by over 11% while the GNP deflator rose by less than 9%. In an inflationary context, the CPI, having fixed base year weights, fails to capture the shift in consumer spending from items whose price has risen rapidly to those whose price has risen more slowly. Thus, for example, higher beef prices since 1972 have induced consumers to shift from beef to poultry and eggs. Higher energy prices have reduced the relative real proportion of outlays devoted to fuels. The CPI, however, assumes that the same real proportion spent in 1972–73 persists. Hence, sharply higher relative prices for such items increase the CPI by more than other indexes that use *current* period weights. As has been said, "pick your market basket and pick your inflation rate."[5] Other differences in the several price indexes lead to further discrepancies in their estimated rates of growth, sometimes as high as three or more percentage points.[6] The "'true'. inflation rate for the economy as a whole depends on which index one chooses to use—each with a different weighting system and a different treatment of certain items, such as housing prices and mortgage rates.

However, on an annual basis, the discrepancies among the indexes are not that large (see table 3.1), and over time the several indexes move in the same direction. Whether the "inflation" rate is 11.3% (CPI) or 8.8% (GNP deflator) when referring to the 1979 increase, does not make all that much difference to one's real standard of living unless perpetuated over a long period of time.

It is also true that all price indexes fail to take account of quality changes in the items we buy. Thus, while the price of automobiles has increased sharply over the last decade, the car we buy in 1980 is not the same as the one purchased in 1970. Presumably, it is better. Depending on the make and model, it may be now more fuel efficient, more comfortable and safe. Government has also mandated that it be less polluting which, while raising its cost and price, may improve the quality of the air we breathe. It is, in any event, different. So it is with many of the foods, drugs, toys, appliances, and clothing we buy. Many of them are "safer." After all, we do have a Consumer Products Safety Commission, a Food and Drug Administration, and so on, that have mandated at least some of these quality changes. Thus, while we pay more now, we *may* be getting better quality and/or longer lives out of some or most of our purchases. To the extent that this is true, a strictly price index will tend to overstate the extent of real price rises. Of course, in some cases, the opposite may be true. We have all suffered from "shoddy workmanship and products" from time to time. Nevertheless on balance, as a guess, if we could adequately measure the quality dimensions of our purchases, it is likely that they have increased. Thus a 2% or even 3% increase in any general price index may in fact represent price stability.

This provides little solace, however, when indexes are rising at 10–18%. Thus, while empirical problems abound in ascertaining the "true" rate of inflation, they cannot possibly account for much of the current inflationary phenomena. Nor is it likely that the rate of increase in the quality dimension has accelerated sharply since the mid-1960s when the U.S. economy not only shifted to a new inflationary plateau but also to (almost) ever-increasing rates for given levels of excess capacity.

Structural Shifts in the Economy

A number of structural changes have occurred in the U.S. economy that may contribute to an explanation of the stagflation problem.

Service Industry Shift

First is the progressive relative shift to a predominantly "service" economy away from an agricultural and "goods-producing" economy. The following table highlights this shift in terms of employment.

Ratio of Employment in Service Industries
To Goods-Producing Industries

Year	
1945	1.31
1950	1.31
1960	1.66
1970	2.02
1979	2.37

Source: *Annual Report of the Council of Economic Advisers*, 1980.

Notes: "Service Industries" include transportation and public utilities, wholesale and retail trade, finance, insurance and real estate, other services and federal, state, and local government. "Goods-Producing Industries" include construction and manufacturing.

The shift of employment out of agriculture has been even more dramatic
—from about 80% of the employed labor force in the nineteenth century to less than 4% at present. As the above table indicates, the relative
importance of the service industries, with respect to employment, is now
about 230% higher than in goods-producing industries.

How does this affect the rate of inflation, especially in the CPI where
services now have a weight of over 40%? The answer in general is quite
straightforward. In goods-producing industries, technological change has
been much greater; hence, productivity increases (that is, output per unit
of resource input, especially labor and capital), have been much greater.
Increased productivity serves to keep down unit labor costs in the goods-
producing sector of the economy even in the face of rising labor costs,
for example. Thus, if output per man-hour rises by, say, 3% per year
overall, money wages could increase by 3% and still yield constant labor
costs per unit of output. In the service sector, on the other hand, productivity is difficult to measure because it is hard to quantify units of
output of doctors', bankers', or professors' services. What in fact do they
produce? Units of health service, units of financial services, units of educational services? How do we measure these? In general, ouput in the
service industries is measured by inputs (say man-hours or value added,
which is heavily weighted by such inputs); hence productivity does not
appear to increase much. Yet wage changes in service industries roughly
parallel those in goods-producing industries. This situation necessarily
imparts an upward bias in the CPI as the economy shifts more and more
to the service sector.

This is, of course, partly a measurement (empirical) problem and partly a structural problem. Nevertheless, it is real and doubtless accounts
in part for both the decrease in productivity of the overall economy in
the last decade (of which much more later) and the upward pressure on
the CPI or any index containing a large and increasing service component.

At the same time, the rapid shift away from agriculture and other
goods-producing industries characterized by relatively large numbers of
producers (and a higher degree of competitiveness) serves naturally to
reduce the degree of downward price flexibility of the economy as a
whole. Such industries exhibit much greater price fluctuations, both up
and down (in the absence of governmentally imposed price fixing), than
more concentrated industries in which prices are "administered" to a far
higher degree. This is discussed more fully below.

Shifts in the Labor Force Composition

The demographic composition of the labor force has shifted quite dramatically away from white males over 20 and increasingly to females, nonwhites, and teenagers (16 to 19 years old). Therefore, an increasing proportion of the labor force is composed of persons whose average productivity is less than white adult males because the relatively large influx is composed of persons whose work experience, skills, and educational levels are, on the average, less than white males. This is true for a variety of reasons, including discriminatory hiring policies in the case of females and nonwhites, recent entrants into the labor force in the case of teenagers and those women who have reentered the labor force after raising a family, lesser amounts and quality of education in the case of nonwhites and some females, and so on.

Over all, although these adverse features can be expected to be overcome in ensuing years, at the time of the heavy influx of new workers during the 1960s and 1970s, the effect was to reduce the average productivity of the employed labor force. This means, on the average, higher unit labor costs, which get passed along more or less quickly in the form of higher prices. Part of the apparent decrease in productivity over the past decade is attributable to this rather profound shift in the composition of the labor force.

But if we seek to explain the high rates of price inflation associated with higher than "normal" rates of unemployment, the changes in the labor force partly account for this as well. That is, unemployment rates for nonwhite adult males are, and have traditionally been, above those of white males. If we look only at the white/nonwhite partition of the labor force, nonwhite unemployment rates have typically been double those of whites. In 1979, for example, the rates were 11.3% and 5.1%, respectively. Adult women (both races) have regularly experienced unemployment rates above those of adult men, although not as strikingly different as the white/nonwhite differential (in 1979 these figures were 5.7% and 4.1%, respectively).[7] Similarly, teenagers as a whole suffer unemployment rates some three to four times higher than adult males (16.1% in 1979 compared with 4.1% for adult males). Nonwhite teenagers have unemployment rates far higher, in the 30–40% range or above in recent years.

If these differentials remain relatively constant over time, the national unemployment rate will inevitably shift higher as the proportion of those typically having higher unemployment rates rises. In short, the full-employment unemployment rate rises as the labor force composition shifts—as it has in the United States over the past 20 to 30 years.

But, in truth, these ratios of minority unemployment rates to adult, male, white unemployment rates have risen in recent years, which compounds the problem even further. We need not venture into the murky sociology of why this may have occurred. Suffice it to say that the combination of the shift of the labor force composition and the rise in the above-mentioned ratios have led many observers to conclude that the full-employment unemployment rate is now in the 6% or even 7% range compared with the 3–4% ranges believed relevant prior to 1965. In other words, the level of output and employment beyond which increases in aggregate demand begin to put severe upward pressure on the price level (the value X_c in figure 3.1) has shifted downwards (to the left along the X axis in figure 3.1). In this way, rates of inflation caused by aggregate demand increases begin to exert their inflationary influence at lower levels of output and employment than previously thought possible.

In addition, higher rates of "normal" unemployment caused by the above phenomena lead to greater total unemployment benefits. These benefits are by definition payments for no current contribution to production. Thus they generate more income and hence expenditure for less output—an inherently inflationary process.

Legal Changes that Contribute to Higher Unemployment

A further factor believed to contribute to the higher unemployment rates of the 1970s, even in the face of high levels of aggregate spending, involves some legal changes made in the early '70s. These include the increase and extension of unemployment insurance benefits as well as changes in the law regarding Aid for Dependent Children and food stamp eligibility. In 1974 and 1976, federal legislation extended both the number of workers covered by unemployment insurance and the number of weeks an unemployed worker could collect such insurance.

For an individual worker, an increase in unemployment benefits means that the cost to him, in terms of wages foregone, is reduced. A reduction in the net cost of unemployment can easily induce the worker to remain unemployed longer, thereby increasing the unemployment rate for the nation as a whole. That is, the national unemployment rate can be construed not only as a weighted average of the unemployment rates of the various groups in the labor force (as noted in the previous section), but also as the average *duration* of unemployment multiplied by the average *frequency* of unemployment.

For example, if the average duration of unemployment is five weeks and if each member of the labor force can be expected to be unemployed once every two years, then the average national unemployment rate is about 4.8% ($\frac{5}{52} \times \frac{1}{2} \cong 4.8\%$). Thus an increase in the amount of compensation will raise the average duration of unemployment, and hence the national average, independently of the level of aggregate demand. Similarly, an extension of the period of coverage from 26 weeks to 65 weeks will operate in the same direction. A worker can "afford" to remain unemployed (or idle) longer—the cost to him has been reduced.

Now all of this unemployment is not necessarily a net loss to society, especially if it permits workers to search longer for better jobs. This permits a closer match between job availability and worker skills. If there were no unemployment compensation, workers might be compelled to take the first job offer that came along, which might be totally unrelated to his or her skills or talents. The importance of this positive aspect of job search cannot be readily quantified.

The evidence of the impact of changes in unemployment insurance on the measured rate of unemployment indicates that this effect is relatively small. Since 1967, the upward bias is believed to be on the order of 0.2% to 0.4%. All other things being equal, the overall unemployment rate of 3.8% recorded in 1967 would therefore have risen to between 4.0% and 4.2% by the late 1970s solely due to changes in the level and extent of unemployment insurance.[8] Several studies indicate that this is a product of both lengthened "job search" and greater frequency of unemployment induced by such changes.[9]

A second factor leading in the same direction is the change in worker registration requirements. Effective 1 July 1972, certain workers were required to register for work to receive food stamps and Aid for Dependent Children. The argument presented by some is that a large number of persons who would not normally be counted as in the labor force are now required to pretend that they are and that they are looking for work. If these persons remain unemployed, this overstates the unemployment rate because the same number is added to both the numerator (the number of unemployed) and the denominator (the size of the civilian labor force). Thus, if the number of unemployed were, say, 5,000,000 out of a labor force of 100,000,000 in a given year, the new registration requirements *may* add an extra million to both totals, thereby increasing the unemployment rate from 5% to almost 6%, again independently of the level of aggregate demand. Some estimates along these lines suggest that the unemployment rate as measured in table 3.2 may overstate the "true" unemployment rate by between one and two percentage points.[10] However, such calculations are extremely difficult to carry out accurately because it is not possible to determine how many of the "new registrants" (the one million in the foregoing example) would not otherwise have been seeking work were it not for the changed requirements in 1972. Other estimates put the impact at between 0.2% to 0.4%, precisely the same as in the case of unemployment insurance.[11] This, of course, illustrates the problems of making empirical estimates of the extent or importance of such impacts. Nonetheless, the general tendency would be in the direction of overstating the "true" amount of unemployment as well as the size of the labor force.

A third factor, whose directional impact is less certain, is the progressive rise in the legal minimum wage rate. This especially affects teenage unemployment. The argument goes that the rise in the teenage unemployment rate relative to that of adult white males is directly related to the successive increases in the minimum wage. Employers may perceive that, at the higher minimum wages, the contributions of relatively unskilled, inexperienced youths may be less than the minimum wage they are obliged to pay. Employers do not rationally employ resources of any kind at a loss.

Offsetting this, in part, is the belief, for which some evidence exists, that the decline in the black teenage labor force participation rate is directly related to the federal minimum wage law. That is, chronic inability to obtain a job may lead to the "discouraged worker" phenomenon and induce many people, especially nonwhite teenagers, simply to withdraw from the labor force and cease looking for work. They are thus not counted as either unemployed or in the labor force. *Deducting* the same amount from both numerator and denominator in the unemployment rate calculation necessarily reduces that rate—just the opposite of the "work requirements" phenomenon noted in the earlier example. On balance, however, it is believed that the *net* impact of the minimum wage laws is to raise the measured unemployment rate, especially of teenagers, by some not inconsiderable extent—perhaps by as much as 4.5%. The effect on the overall national unemployment rate, using estimates from 1956 to 1974, is to raise it by 0.63%. But there are many ambiguities in the data, and all the authors of these studies suggest they be used with caution.[12]

Various, often valiant, attempts have been made to measure these fluctuations in the work force. However, the calculations are subject to many doubts and reservations. We need not review this literature here.

The general conclusion is that there is little doubt that these legal and structural changes mean that the full-employment unemployment rate (or the "natural" rate of unemployment) is higher than it was earlier. This, in turn, means that, whereas in the past an unemployment rate of 3–4% was consistent with relative price stability, now a rate closer to 5% or 6% is "normal." Attempts to push the unemployment rate much below 6% therefore lead to higher rates of inflation. It is as if the aggregate supply curve of figure 3.1 began to turn upward sharply at some considerable distance to the left of X_1. The Phillips curve has in essence shifted outward and become more vertical. Some of the present stagflation is doubtless attributable to the phenomena related to the labor force which cause prices to rise sharply long before unemployment rates of 3–4% are achieved by monetary and fiscal policies or by other factors affecting aggregate demand.

But there are yet other reasons for believing that inflationary pressures can exist even when aggregate demand is not excessive. To these we now turn.

The Role of Industrial Structure

I have presented above the main reasons for believing that higher rates of unemployment or higher degrees of excess capacity may have been required for price stability in the last 15 years than was earlier required. There still remains the question of how inflationary pressures can be generated even with rates of unemployment above 6%. Note that in 1975 with unemployment running at 8.5%, the CPI increased by 9.1%, the worst performance in any of the past 30 years. However, 1980 promises to be even worse in terms of the "discomfort" index, with inflation expected to run at about 12% for the year as a whole and the unemployment rate at 7–8%. Such a poor performance cannot be satisfactorily explained by any of the longer term structural features noted in previous sections. Even if the "true" unemployment rate is overstated by 2%, this still implies a discomfort index of 17 to 18%—a rate far too high to tolerate with equanimity.

The main explanations of rising prices, even with a deficiency of aggregate spending, are rooted in market imperfections. The argument is that the U.S. economy is composed of two types of nonregulated industry. One is highly monopolistic (automobiles, steel, oil, aluminum, etc.) and often dominated by one or two very large firms (General Motors, IBM, Western Electric, General Electric, Xerox, Exxon, etc.—generally those in the *Fortune* "500"). The other sector is more highly competitive on a price basis and is composed of relatively small firms (much of agriculture, many of the service and retailing industries and some manufacturing).

In the less competitive or monopolistic sector, the responses of the firms to a decrease in the demand for their products is not a reduction of prices. These firms fear that this may generate further price decreases by their few rivals and initiate a price "war" resulting in serious revenue losses to all concerned. Tacit or often explicit agreements of various types *not* to compete on a price basis are believed to prevail in highly concentrated industries. In addition, for larger firms, managerial strategy may be to maintain relative price stability for the sake of customer relations and not to exploit fully short-run profit potential when demand rises but to maintain prices when demand decreases. Many firms also price on the basis of markups over unit production costs. If such costs do not fall much when demand and output decrease, prices will be held higher than in markets in which supply and demand forces function more fully—that is, markets continuously being cleared by price fluctuations. Indeed, for many firms with large elements of costs that do not vary much in response to changes in output, a reduction in production *raises* unit costs. Hence, the preservation of any percentage markup requires a price *increase* despite a demand decrease. When costs are rising due to higher prices for raw materials or wage rates, prices will promptly be raised even if demand is falling. Thus the response to a decrease in demand is the slowing of the rate of production rather than the lowering of prices. This means reduced purchases of inputs such as labor and raw materials, which in turn adds to unemployment with stable, rigid, or even rising prices.

For firms in more competitive industries, a decrease in demand directly leads to price reductions because the relatively large number of firms does not have a recognized mutual interdependence. Price reductions may also result because tacit or formal agreements with respect to price are harder to come by as the number of firms in any industry grows. At the extreme in a perfect auction market, all firms are price takers and must accept a market-determined price responsive to the free forces of supply and demand in that market. In such industries, therefore, the brunt of any decrease in demand is borne by price decreases and conversely with increased demand. Such markets exhibit a high degree of both downward and upward price sensitivity in response to shifting demands and costs. This contrasts to the downward price *rigidity* of monopolistic enterprises or enterprises not operating in auction markets.

The stage is now set for an explanation of stagflation—high and rising prices in the face of high and rising unemployment for the nation as a whole. Even if aggregate spending is not excessive, or even when aggregate demand is decreasing, beneath the aggregate, demands for the products of specific industries are constantly shifting—some increasing, others decreasing. If the demand decreases are heavily concentrated in the monopolistic industries, prices will not fall, but output and employment will. On the other hand, wherever demand increases, in either competitive or monopolistic industries, prices will rise, albeit to different degrees. The net effect is to raise the general level of prices (downwardly rigid prices in some industries but upward price flexibility in others), while increasing the level of unemployment over all.

There are, of course, many problems, analytical and empirical, in this schematic discussion. Unemployment, over all, will rise only if the employment reductions (layoffs) in the monopolistic industries exceed the employment increases in the industries experiencing an increase in demand. This would be likely if the reduction in employment is regionally specific (say, in the automobile industry in Michigan) but the demand increases occur in other parts of the country. Labor is not mobile, especially in the short run, because of moving costs, nonvested pension rights, unemployment compensation, lack of knowledge of jobs elsewhere, lack of jobs consistent with the skills of those laid off, and so forth.

Nor is it inevitable that downward demand shifts are concentrated in monopolistic industries. If they are significantly concentrated in more competitive industries, prices in general should fall, and unemployment should increase little, if at all.

Nevertheless, as a possible explanation of how prices can rise despite considerable overall slack in the economy, the above, often referred to as the "demand-shift" explanation of stagflation, has considerable merit. Indeed, there is much evidence of the differential price behavior of these two broad sectors. However, demand-shift cannot explain the deteriorating performance of the U.S. economy over the past 15 years, for there is no evidence that the U.S. economy has become significantly more concentrated or monopolistic since the end of World War II. Thus, this hypothesis cannot explain why stagflation did not become a problem earlier. Indeed, defining degrees of competitiveness for specific industries is a hazardous occupation. But it does suggest that we could well strive to reduce the degree of downward price inflexibility wherever it exists in the economy. Such a reduction could be effected by a more vigorous enforcement of the antitrust laws to prevent the more formal types of price agreement among firms as well as by an alteration in the industrial structure. The latter is no easy task, but attempting to remove barriers to entry, permitting easier imports of competing products (foreign cars, steel, TV sets, and the like), would help.

The evidence does, however, suggest that the U.S. economy has become increasingly insensitive to downward overall price level adjustments in the face of deficiencies of aggregate demand. Thus, in the ten business cycles between 1891 and 1929, the average rate of increase of the Wholesale Price Index (now the Producer Price Index) was less than 4%, whereas prices fell in nine of the cycles by more than 4% during the downswing. However, during the four business cycles between 1949 and 1970, the price index rose during both the upswing and downswing.[13] In the sharper recession of 1974–75, all price indexes rose, and they are rising during the slump of 1980.

A variant of the demand-shift argument is that of "cost-push." Even though there may be a deficiency of total spending, certain industries may face rising costs due to sharp increases in the prices of raw materials (oil, for example) or due to pressures for higher real wages from organized labor. If the industries and the firms therein have a certain degree of monopoly power, and if sales are not very sensitive to prices, such cost increases will be passed along in the form of higher prices. If this is a one-shot cost and price increase, it cannot generate an inflation *process* unless the industries so affected produce inputs used by other industries —inputs that, in turn, raise prices in those industries, and so on. Alternatively, those workers obtaining higher wages will create incentives for other workers to, in a sense, catch up. Or if the initial price rise substantially affects the CPI, other workers will either demand higher wages to maintain their purchasing power or obtain them automatically if wages are indexed. Thus may begin a process of escalating costs, wages, and prices induced by a single pervasive supply-side shock of the type we have experienced as a result of the OPEC cartel in 1973 and continued subsequent oil price increases. However, if aggregate demand remains low, the process may not continue for long as companies facing declining demand refuse to agree to higher wages or decrease their demands for the more costly inputs. The length of time it takes to end the inflation process, however, may be quite long and the costs in terms of unemployment and output foregone very high indeed.

Conditions in Labor Markets

The inflationary process so initiated may be further enhanced by what has been referred to as "the invisible handshake"[14] and the "job queue."[15] Both of these notions argue that wage deflation will not occur in most labor markets, even if there is a large excess supply of labor and innumerable applicants for specific jobs. Indeed, as we have witnessed during the 1970s, employers (both union and nonunion) have regularly granted general pay increases without much regard to the number of applicants for the available positions. Nor in most large businesses is it any longer possible to obtain employment by offering to work for less. Indeed, in the context of the inflationary pressures of the past decade, not only do workers expect money wages to rise at least by the amount of inflation, but most employers in fact grant raises with or without formal contracts specifying regular cost-of-living adjustments.

In labor markets and in many commodity markets, there has arisen what might be termed "implicit contracts." Certainly, the wage rate in specific markets is not adjusted daily or even weekly in response to changes in supply and demand conditions in the same way that the commodity markets, foreign exchange, and stock markets adjust. The employment relationship is much more stable than fluctuations in output largely because the brunt of supply and demand change is not allowed to alter wages and prices to the full extent needed to "clear the market." Especially in labor markets, wages are often negotiated. But even where they are not (and nonunion markets still account for about three-fourths of the U.S. economy), employers do not take advantage of every excess supply of workers to reduce wages.

In addition to a strong element of equity, fairness, and comparison with wages in other industries (along with institutional inertia), this phenomenon is reinforced by rational economic considerations. The implicit contract not to reduce wage rates at every opportunity, to maintain long-term employment relations and a decent work environment in which workers can expect a rising standard of living, is also rooted in cost considerations. Labor turnover costs are relatively high. A company without a perceived record of "decent" wages and a relatively stable employment pattern would have a difficult and costly time rehiring equally efficient workers when demand for its product increased following a wage reduction and/or extensive layoffs. Furthermore, many employers invest heavily in manpower training or in on-the-job training. Some of the training may even be company-specific. Such workers, subject to regular layoffs or recurrent wage reductions every time demand decreased, would be reluctant to return to the same employer. As many of the large employers in Japan have discovered, there are real productivity and loyalty payoffs to "lifetime employment."

On the other side of the implicit labor contract, wages do not rise immediately each time production is increased. Yet they do tend to rise in response to inflationary pressures to maintain real purchasing power—and indeed they rise somewhat more in response to productivity increases and/or pressures to increase real living standards.

In this way, any sharp production cost increases, such as the more than doubling of world oil prices between January 1978 and January 1979, have the effect of spilling over into the CPI (during 1979 it was estimated that the index increased 2.25% as a direct result of higher energy prices).[16] As the Council of Economic Advisors (CEA) put it:

> Temporary excess demand or sharply rising food and energy prices would not affect the inflation for more than a limited period if they did not become built into longer-term trend rates of increase in wages and other costs. However, as outside shocks drive up materials prices, business may seek to maintain profit margins by raising prices. The higher prices of finished goods may induce workers to try to protect their real incomes by demanding larger nominal wages. . . . Temporary shocks that aggravate inflation can thus become imbedded in underlying inflation.[17]

Thus, conditions in the labor market and many product and service markets make the economy uniquely susceptible to so-called supply-side shocks in initiating an inflationary process. This is especially true when the shocks themselves persist, as has been the case with OPEC's oil prices since 1973.

The Role of Foreign Trade

As a manifestation of the increasing world economic interdependence, of which we hear so much, U.S. imports have increased in current values approximately fivefold in the last decade. As a proportion of GNP, they have doubled in current values. The bulk of this represents price increases for the goods and services purchased from abroad. In fact, in constant dollars of 1972, "real" imports rose by only 60% (not 500%) and, as a proportion of GNP, increased from only 5.89% in 1969 to 7.15% in 1979.

The import bill has thus increased sharply due to price rises abroad. This increase raises the prices not only of raw materials and other productive imports but also of consumer goods imports, both of which have increasingly affected the U.S. price level during the 1970s.

The failure of U.S. exports to rise as rapidly (in current values) increases the U.S. foreign trade deficit and adversely affects the balance of payments as well. This, in turn, puts downward pressure on the value of the dollar vis-à-vis other currencies. Thus the dollar was deliberately devalued twice under the Nixon Administration and has sunk even further relative to most European and Japanese currencies under the floating exchange rate systems.

Such devaluations obviously increase the dollar costs of everything imported from nations against which the dollar has depreciated. They also provide OPEC and other oil exporting nations with an excuse to raise oil prices for precisely the same rationale as labor uses for wage increases designed to maintain their living standards, since oil is priced in terms of dollars. In addition, as foreign nations come to believe that the United States will be unable to contain its domestic inflation (i.e., that the purchasing power of their dollar holdings will diminish relative to other currencies for nations whose domestic inflation is less—for instance, West Germany and Japan), there is a strong inducement to exchange dollars for, say, marks or yen, thus creating an excess supply of dollars in the foreign exchange markets. This exerts even more downward pressure on the value of the dollar. This devaluation exacerbates U.S. inflation and reinforces the belief that it will not be contained—a kind of vicious circle leading to self-perpetuating inflationary pressures from the foreign trade sector.

Thus, beyond supply side shocks, generated by the increasingly perceived shortage of important metals, minerals, and foodstuffs (often leading to large price increases in competitive or cartelized foreign markets), the high deficits in the U.S. trade balance and the huge dollar deposits held abroad (in, say, the Eurodollar markets) lead to sharp downward pressures on the value of the dollar. These pressures, in turn, exacerbate both domestic U.S. inflation and the balance of trade.

To be sure, the increased supply of foreign goods, if at stable prices, should offset inflationary pressures for any given level of aggregate demand. But, as we have seen, the value of imports has risen mainly due to higher prices. In competitive domestic markets, these increased prices would normally be expected to reduce imports. However, many of the domestic markets are not highly competitive, and some U.S. producers have used the higher import prices of their foreign competitors as an umbrella to raise domestic prices as well. Thus foreign automobiles have captured higher shares of the U.S. market (in terms of number of cars), despite rising prices.

Another effect of the rising foreign trade deficits should be to *reduce* aggregate demand. If exports minus imports are negative, this reduces nominal GNP which should put downward pressure on the domestic price level—other things being equal, as economists are prone to say. However, it is apparent from the previous paragraph that other things are far from equal. In terms of figure 3.1, it is clear that the aggregate supply function has been shifting upward faster than aggregate demand has shifted downward, as a result of the negative balance of trade—the cost and price impacts have exceeded the demand impacts as far as the foreign sector is concerned. Indeed, large as the foreign trade deficits have been in the United States since 1976, as a proportion of GNP they are minuscule (e.g., $4.6 billion in 1979 compared with a GNP in 1979 of $2,369 billion). Hence, their negative impact on total U.S. spending is relatively insignificant.

The Role of Expectations

When an economy experiences higher rates of inflation for a sustained period of time, consumers, workers, and businesses will come to anticipate at least its perpetuation. Depending on the nature of the rate of change of inflation (whether steady, accelerating, decreasing, or variable),[18] these three (overlapping) groups will expect the inflation rate to stay the same, rise, fall, or continue to vary, depending on current and expected circumstances. Such expectations can have profound effects on the actual course of inflation.

For example, suppose consumers in general believe that prices will continue to increase for the market basket of commodities "normally" purchased (or purchased in some base period). For "essential" commodities needed on a regular basis (e.g., food), there is little choice, although substitution possibilities exist (for example, purchases may shift to a lower grade or quality of particular items). But for postponable items, such as consumer durables, the anticipation of higher prices has the effect of accelerating their current acquisition, if it is also expected that real incomes will not decrease. The syndrome of "buy now before a rise in prices of those things that will be necessary in the future," operates with full force. In a society in which real incomes have regularly risen, this effect tends to predominate. If so, then personal consumption expenditures will tend to rise, which will reinforce inflationary pressures for any given level of capacity of the economy to produce. The sharp reduction in the household savings ratio over the last several years attests to this attempt to maintain real living standards in the face of anticipated inflation.

In the case of anticipated accelerating inflation, this ultimately gives rise to the "spend your income as fast as you can" syndrome, which typifies galloping inflation of the German type examined in chapter 2. In terms of figure 3.1, aggregate demand keeps rising at a rate continually faster than the productive capacity of the economy to produce. The price level therefore rises at an accelerating rate, savings dwindle, and needed investment cannot be financed except by accelerating increases in the money supply or the velocity of circulation—of which more later.

On the other hand, if nominal household income is not expected to rise, increased purchases of essentials reduce the discretionary income and may induce a *reduction* in purchases of postponable items. Households can utilize their existing automobiles, refrigerators, appliances, and even clothing over a longer time period than they usually do. Thus nominal spending on such items may drop at the same time that nominal spending on "essentials" rises. The former represents a real reduction in demand for durables, while the latter represents no real change. In short, the role of inflationary expectations can result in rising unemployment in durable goods industries, including automobiles and housing, with no increase in employment in other industries. Inflation, in short, can *cause* overall unemployment. For example, the sharp increase in oil prices in late 1973 from about $2.75/bbl to over $10 was analogous to a tax on the U.S. consumer of some $35 billion in the aggregate, and this greatly reduced household discretionary income for spending on other things. Instead of a trade-off between inflation and unemployment, the one may be a cause of the other if nominal incomes do not rise to compensate. This is especially true of sharp price increases from foreign sources, since these reduce nominal U.S. income and require substitution among household purchases along the lines noted above.

If labor as a whole also anticipates continued inflation, it will demand nominal wage increases at least equal to the expected inflation rate, if only to maintain the existing standard of living. Even in hard-pressed, nonunionized industries, wage increases are likely to be granted or even offered. Annual wage increases have become a way of life in the U.S. economy ever since World War II either as a reward for "loyalty," productivity, to offset inflation, or on grounds of equity à la the "invisible handshake" noted earlier.

But if the rate of inflation during the next period is expected to be, say, 8%, any money wage increase less than this will be considered a decrease and will be staunchly resisted or resented. In addition, employees accustomed to rising real standards of living will request, on top of the inflation factor, the normal "productivity" increment in the range of about 3–4%. Finally, it is to be expected that wage demands or requests above these two sums will be made for bargaining purposes, to compensate for the failure of the last wage increase to reflect productivity, inflation, and/or equity factors.

Thus labor, whether organized or not, will demand, request, or expect wage increases in the 15% range if inflation expectations are in the 8–10% range.

If business firms also expect inflation in the 8–10% range and believe that price increases for *their* product can be greater than this—or, indeed, that granting a 15% wage increase would "justify" price hikes higher than the inflation rate to their customers—there is a strong likelihood that wages overall will be increased close to labor's expectations, themselves significantly increased by widely held inflationary expectations.

CONCLUSION

In short, a wide variety of changes in the economy has produced a situation in which prices as a whole are far freer to rise than to fall. As Haberler put it (as long ago as 1966),

> The country is more sensitive to inflation than it used to be in earlier periods. There is now a history of creeping inflation more than 30 years long—secular inflation, one is tempted to say. By this I mean the fact that since 1932 the price level has never gone down. The price picture, which for earlier periods was that of a wave, has become one of an ascending staircase. Periods of rising prices are separated by plateaus of uneasy stability and not by periods of declining prices.[19]

This has become even more evident since 1966. Indeed, the staircase or "ratchet" effect of the price level has antecedents dating back to 1300, according to the price index for Southern England, noted in chapter 2.

Absent from the foregoing set of factors that cause or contribute to stagflation and to the worsening trade-off between unemployment and inflation is the role of government in this process. In the absence of governmental policies, one could (and many have) plausibly argue that sharply rising prices would lower the real value of money holdings (cash or checking account deposits or savings accounts). The reduction of, say, real household monetary assets will hold down consumption spending as people attempt to rebuild the value of their asset base. But if the monetary authorities increase the money supply, this effect will not take place. The inflation can, in short, be validated by public policy. Similarly, if the unemployment rate rises "too much," both monetary and fiscal policies will try to reverse the situation by stimulating aggregate demand, by tax reductions and the like, which in turn will validate the inflationary forces. Any attempt to push the unemployment rate below its so-called natural rate, itself hard to define with much precision, will generate a further round of price increases, rekindle inflationary expectations, and so on. The commitment to a policy of full employment—no matter how the latter is measured, in the face of the various structural, expectational, and other changes. or circumstances noted in this chapter— clearly leads to an inflationary bias.

But it is not only through the use of monetary and fiscal policies that the federal government may aggravate the inflationary process. Economic regulation of some key industries (e.g., transportation and communications) reduces competition within these industries, raises their costs, and thus imparts a higher level of downward price rigidity than would otherwise exist. Minimum wage laws, price support programs, and so on, work in the same direction, as do sales and excise taxes, unemployment compensation, tariffs, and quotas on imports. Many of these measures are more or less legitimate—or at least understandable—responses to particular problems. They do, however, contribute to inflationary forces, regardless of their other merits. Nor is there much point in arguing that if we created enough unemployment and persisted in policies of restraining aggregate demand "long enough," the inflation rate would decrease. No one knows how long is "long enough." It may take many years of unemployment rates over 7%— some argue over 10%. Such unemployment would be an intolerable waste of human talent and output, especially in a political democracy. Nor does it make much sense to fight inflation with policies that *restrict*

4 The Role of Government

INTRODUCTION

Since the Great Depression—and especially since World War II—all Western-style democracies have adopted activist policies designed to ensure that aggregate demand in the economy was high enough to yield satisfactory levels of employment. After the Keynesian revolution in economics, the indirect manipulative tools of monetary and fiscal policy were viewed as the primary instruments needed to achieve a higher degree of overall stability of the economic system, as discussed in the previous chapter. Indeed, the Employment Act of 1946 in the United States asserted that it was one of the duties of the federal government to ensure consistently high levels of employment along with stable prices. A Great Depression was never to occur again! By skillful adaptation of federal taxation and expenditures, and with the Federal Reserve System's careful management of the money supply, it was thought that major cyclical movements of the economy could be prevented.

With a lot of luck, some reasonably good management, but especially the development of certain "automatic stabilizers,"[1] as well as the resilience and adaptability of the private sector to rapid population growth, technological change, and increased foreign competition, the U.S. economy grew rapidly.[2] In constant dollars of 1972, real GNP increased from $533.5 billion in 1950 to $1,431.6 billion in 1979, a compound annual average rate of growth of almost 4% per year. Perhaps even more remarkable is that only six recessions occurred during this 29-year period with only four of them showing up in year-to-year declines in real GNP. Furthermore, the declines in real output and the accompanying increases in unemployment were relatively mild. The largest year-to-year decline in real GNP was −1.4% in 1974. A statistical comparison of the Great Depression with the most severe recession following it (that of 1974–75) is given in table 4.1.

Noteworthy in this table is the extremely sharp decline in the GNP and all its components (except government GNP purchases) in 1929–1933,

TABLE 4.1

A Comparison of the "Great Depression"
with the "Recession" of 1974-75

Item	1929	1933	% Change	1973 IV	1975 II	% Change
GNP ($ billions 1958)	204	142	− 30	845	784	− 7.2
P.C.E. "	140	113	− 19	521	510	− 2
G.P.D.I. "	40	5	− 88	135	80	−41
Government GNP Purchases	22	23	+ 5	180	184	+ 2
Disposable Personal Income* (current $)	(83)	(46)	− 45	(918)	(1,079)	+15
Unemployment rate (%)	3.2	24.9		4.7	8.7	
Employment (millions)	48	39	− 19	86	84	− 2
Hourly Earnings in Mfg. ($)*	0.56	0.44	− 21	4.17	4.74	+12
Weekly Earnings in Mfg. ($)*	25	17	− 32	169	186	+ 9
Index of Industrial Production (1967 = 100)	22	14	− 36	127	110	−13
New Housing Starts (000)	509	93	− 82	1,484	1,305	−12
Business Failures (000)	23	32	+ 39	740	1,045	+29
Consumer Price Index* (1967 = 100)	51	39	− 24	138	145	+ 5
Interest Rate on Prime Commercial Paper (%)	5.9	1.7		8.9	5.8	
Corporate Profits (billions, before taxes)	11	−1	−109	69	67	− 3

Note: Starred (*) items indicate divergent movements in the series between the two contractions.
Source: Council of Economic Advisers, Annual Reports, various years.

compared with 1973 IV–1975 II (the peak to trough periods). The decline in real total output in the Great Depression was more than four times that of the next worst recession (1974–75). The duration of all postwar recessions has also been very short in comparison, the recession of 1980 being the shortest of all. The role of the built-in or automatic stabilizers (reduced tax receipts when income falls, combined with higher unemployment compensation) is also indicated in the behavior of disposable (i.e., after tax) personal income. Disposable income dropped some 45% between 1929 and 1933, but actually rose 15% in the later recession. Thus, in comparison with the Great Depression, consumption was sustained fairly well in the more recent slump.

The disturbing part, to which I alluded earlier, is that both wages and prices (as measured by the CPI) continued to rise during the 1974–75 recession. This contrasts sharply with the earlier prewar period.

Viewed in historical perspective, the U.S. economy is now remarkably recession-proof. Part of this is due to the federal government's far greater willingness and ability to reduce tax rates to stimulate the economy at the outset of a recession. In 1932, on the other hand, President Hoover proposed and a Democratically-controlled Congress enacted the largest peacetime tax *increase*, largely in a vain attempt to balance the budget— such was the prevailing orthodoxy. In addition, the Federal Reserve System allowed the money supply to *contract* (some 33%) *after* the onset of the Depression. In the face of a strong downturn in economic activity, the Federal Reserve System has not acted so perversely since.[3]

Other antirecession safeguards such as deposit insurance, unemployment insurance, higher progressivity of the income tax structure, mortgage guarantees, and so on, reinforce the willingness to take actions that are at least not perverse in the fiscal and monetary arenas. The rewriting of a portion of received economic analysis along Keynesian lines provided analytical support for such willingness. It may not quite be true that "we are all Keynesians now," as Milton Friedman was reported to have sadly proclaimed following the apparent success of the Kennedy tax cut reduction in 1964[4]—which was designed not so much to offset actual or incipient recession but mainly to raise the then sluggish growth rate. It is nevertheless true that the Keynesian analysis and prescriptions were, until recently, widely accepted in the economics profession and by all governments of the Western world.[5] To be sure, recent attacks on the *ability* of activist fiscal and monetary policies to influence the economy significantly, especially when it comes to inflation (the so-called rational expectations hypothesis), have somewhat blurred the Keynesian approach. And, certainly, there was never any guarantee that activist policies would be pursued intelligently, especially in the political sphere.

Nevertheless, the Keynesian message has been effectively absorbed. Its comparative effectiveness is illustrated, though not proved, by the paucity of recessions since World War II, as well as their comparative mildness and short duration. The same, however, cannot be said about its applicability to situations of inflation, especially in the context of stagflation or the expectations-augmented Phillips curve. Experience since the late 1960s—and especially the late 1970s—suggests that something more (or less!) than even sensibly applied monetary and fiscal policy may be required to extricate ourselves from the "stagflation swamp," as Arthur Okun so aptly put it.

In order to understand some of these issues and the role of government, let us examine the problems involved in implementing monetary and fiscal policy.

PROBLEMS OF IMPLEMENTATION OF SENSIBLE
MONETARY AND FISCAL POLICY

Even if we still lived in a Keynesian world, a world in which inflation was solely caused by spending too much and unemployment was solely caused by spending too little, some more or less serious problems would emerge in sensible implementation of monetary and fiscal policies designed to control the total level of spending. In the non-Keynesian world already sketched, these problems are even more difficult. However, let us assume a Keynesian world. What are some of the difficulties?

The Primacy of Economic Goals

The goals of any society encompass much more than economic efficiency, steady noninflationary growth, full employment, and equilibrium balance of payments. To be sure, achievement of such goals contributes to other, more fundamental goals. As Heller put it,

> the term "full employment" stands as a proxy . . . for the fulfillment of the individual as a productive member of society, for the greater equality of giving every able-bodied worker access to a job. . . . *Rapid economic growth* [is] our proxy for a rising standard and quality of life at home, and an ever-broadening base for our economic and political leadership abroad. *Price stability* [is] our proxy for equity between fixed and variable income recipients and, in today's outward-looking economy, a vital condition for maintaining our competitive position in world markets without trade restriction. *Balance-of-payments equilibrium* [is] our proxy for promoting an international setting in which there will be free movement of people, commerce, and finance across national boundaries, and free scope for expansionary domestic policies.[6]

But many of these interrelationships between economic goals and noneconomic values are tenuous at best. From time to time, the federal government may be compelled to run large deficits, even in the face of inflationary prospects. Thus, in World War II, the military needs took precedence over anti-inflation policies. It was simply not possible to reduce nonmilitary expenditures enough to offset the impact of rapidly rising military outlays required to defeat Germany and Japan. Nor was it deemed feasible to raise taxes by the amounts needed to balance the budget in an inflationary situation—largely due to the disincentive impact on output. Thus, the always clumsy expedients of price controls and rationing were resorted to. More recently, the apparent necessity of raising military spending, in the wake of the failure of detente and the Soviet invasion of Afghanistan, increased government spending more than policymakers would have desired for stabilization purposes, at least prior to the onset of a contraction in early 1980 that was sharper than anyone had forecast.

Often societies perceive particular needs as having an exceptional urgency independent of their potentially adverse macroeconomic effects. It is, of course, desirable to mitigate their adverse effects to whatever extent possible. But it is not always possible to mitigate these effects completely, especially where national security issues are involved. Even where such issues are not involved, however, there are frequently important trade-offs and risks that are, it is felt, worth taking. For example, suppose we reach a goal of reasonably full employment, which would call for at least a balanced government budget and some monetary restraint. One could still argue that increased spending, or lower taxes and interest rates designed to push the unemployment rate even lower, would create more job opportunities for the poor and the disadvantaged. The values of these measures might well justify the risk of increased inflationary pressures, especially if such action would serve to temper urban riots and other forms of disruption by a frustrated minority denied access to employment. Since no solid, cast-iron measure of the full-employment unemployment rate exists, this option is very appealing to policymakers with a keen sense of social injustice.

Nor does economic success, however measured, necessarily produce "happiness" or a "decent" society. Economic success *permits* any society to do more things but says absolutely nothing about the kinds of things actually done. Nazi Germany could not have committed many of its misdeeds during the 1930s and early 1940s without a fairly high degree of economic achievement—nor could Japan during World War II. Economic achievement may well be a prerequisite to a high level of civilization but, as Keynes remarked many years ago, it is no guarantee. The regularly recurring concern with the "quality of life" suggests that high and rising levels of per capita GNP are no golden keys to social tranquility, individual fulfillment, or a clean natural environment. At the same time, there is nothing personally or socially elevating about poverty or falling output. Given a choice, it is better to have higher per capita incomes than lower. The point is that the former does not necessarily lead to the happy life, however defined. The *composition* of GNP—the kinds of things we produce—may therefore be, in some value sense, of higher importance than the aggregate referred to as GNP.

Yet these philosophical musings should not deter us from our attempt to achieve reasonable macroeconomic goals. Indeed, Keynesian economics was and is an attempt to preserve the advantages of a predominantly free enterprise system by methods consistent with Western values. The alternative is some form of monolithic state system à la Hitler or Stalin, or a degree of overall and detailed planning that may adversely affect efficiency and private incentives. Thus, while economics is far from everything, it is far beyond nothing. If the enterprise system is inherently unstable in the presence of a passive central government policy stressing balanced budgets and monetary change to "accommodate" commerce, then some activist (i.e., responsive) policy by the central government is essential. What Keynes tried to provide is basically a non-Marxist solution to the problem of cyclical instability, consistent with the goals of efficiency and individualism.

The advantages of free enterprise, as Keynes put it in 1936, are

> the advantages of decentralisation and the play of self-interest. The advantage to efficiency of the decentralisation of decisions and of individual responsibility is even greater, perhaps, than the nineteenth century supposed. . . . But, above all, individualism, if it can be purged of its defects and abuses [i.e., instability], is the best safeguard of personal liberty in the sense that, compared with any other system, it greatly widens the field for the exercise of personal choice. . . . Whilst, therefore, the enlargement of the functions of government involved in the task of adjusting to one another the propensity to consume and the inducement to invest [i.e., controlling total spending], would seem to a nineteenth-century publicist or to a contemporary American financier to be a terrific encroachment on individualism, I defend it, on the contrary, both as the only practicable means of avoiding the destruction of existing economic forms in their entirety and as the condition of the successful functioning of individual initiative.[7]

Thus, sensible use of monetary and fiscal policy remains high on both the social and economic agenda of all Western-oriented nations. Conservatives as well as liberals can surely accept this as a minimum. If so, then some of the problems of effectively implementing monetary and fiscal policy need to be squarely faced, even in the assumed Keynesian world. Indeed, these contribute to the present problems confronting both U.S. and world economies.

Persistence of Economic Myths

One of the tenets of activist fiscal policy is that in times of actual or incipient recession the federal government should run at a deficit and, on the other hand, run a surplus during actual or incipient inflation.

The former would mitigate the recession while the latter would mitigate inflation. However, the accepted principles of public finance inherited from the nineteenth century insist that, in order to balance the budget annually, the government should live within its means just as individuals are constrained to do.

At the same time, monetary policy, to the extent that it ever was a policy, during the 1920s accepted as its role that of "accommodating commerce." Thus, when economic activity was at a low level, the money supply should have been contracted and, conversely, expanded when economic activity was brisk.

As noted earlier in this chapter, adherence to such principles aggravated the Great Depression. Yet it should (now) be obvious that insistence on an annually balanced budget would aggravate cyclical swings, as would the "accommodate commerce" approach to money supply regulation. For example, especially with a progressive income tax system, when economic expansion is taking place, government revenues rise. To balance the budget, then, requires either that government expenditures increase or that tax rates decrease, thereby accelerating the expansion of total spending and contributing to inflation. Conversely, when the economy is contracting, government tax receipts decline, which, if the budget is to balance, requires an increase in tax rates and/or a decrease in government spending, each of which accelerates the contraction. An annually balanced federal government budget thus aggravates instability rather than offsets it.[8]

The essence of the Keynesian message was to use fiscal and, to a lesser extent, monetary policy to *offset* cyclical instability. Thus, deficits should be run in the face of actual or incipient contraction, and surpluses when inflationary pressures existed or appeared imminent.

But the nineteenth century's canons of fiscal and monetary responsibility persisted. Indeed, they have recently made a comeback with President Carter's and President Reagan's unattainable "goal" of a balanced budget in 1981. We should remember, however, that circumstances at the time appeared somewhat rational, and that the Fed insisted on monetary restraint.

The deeply felt importance of a regularly balanced budget, however economically irrational, obviously impeded an activist fiscal policy. Members of Congress tend to reflect such strongly held beliefs, thus making it difficult for any president to enact legislation designed to produce a deficit or even a surplus. The widespread belief persevered that a federal deficit somehow reflected a failure—analogous to a business firm's loss.

Even Presidents Roosevelt and Kennedy, activists both, originally sought a balanced budget.

In reality, there is no analogy between a business loss and a federal government deficit because the bookkeeping methods differ drastically between the public and private sectors. In public accounting at the federal level, there is no charge for depreciation of public assets. In addition, all expenditures, whether for capital or current purposes, are lumped together. Any private corporation that is expanding via capital investments would inevitably show sizeable losses if it did not allocate its investment outlays over some anticipated lifetime. Since there is no valid analogy between deficits in the public sector and business losses (nor between business profits and public sector surpluses), there is no reason to celebrate a surplus in the federal budget, nor lament a deficit.

Why doesn't the government adopt business accounting procedures? These procedures are designed accurately to measure business profits whereas the government is not in "business" to make a profit. If it were, it could raise taxes sharply and spend little—a situation that would please few and have large economic implications, usually adverse. Furthermore, the rate of depreciation or amortization of public expenditures on capital account is difficult to determine on other than arbitrary grounds. Indeed, the very distinction between current and capital spending is arbitrary. How does one treat military expenditures, even those giving rise to missile bases or other physical structures? These expenditures are as difficult to distinguish as are current and capital outlays—so it is with public parks or other recreational facilities, not to mention roads, schools, and hospitals. Many governments make, or try to make, distinctions between current (or above-the-line) expenditures and capital (or below-the-line) expenditures, but the arbitrariness of such distinctions has induced the U.S. federal government, at least, not to do so. In this sense, U.S. public accounting is more honest.

But does not a deficit, however computed, lead to a higher national debt? Of course it does. To finance a deficit, the government, like any business enterprise, must issue securities. When issued by the federal government, these become part of the national debt, interest and principal (when due) on which has to be paid, which may be burdensome, depending on who holds the debt. Once again, however, the widespread equation between a private debt and national debt needs to be examined.

If the bulk of the national debt is held by citizens of the nation, as in the case with the U.S. national debt, interest and principal payments on the debt represent an income or wealth transfer between taxpayers and bondholders. On the other hand, if a large portion of the national debt is held by foreigners, the U.S. economy bears a real burden in the sense that part of each year's GNP must be used to satisfy foreign debt claims against the United States; fewer goods and services then remain to be consumed by U.S. citizens. The foreign debt presently incurred by many non-oil-producing poor countries seriously impedes their growth prospects.

Even in the case of an internally held debt, there are still some consequences that may be adverse or beneficial. Taxpayers and bondholders do not uniquely coincide. Some income redistribution will therefore occur within the economy. Since it is generally the relatively more affluent who hold government (or any) securities, while the tax system is fairly ubiquitous, income inequality will increase somewhat by virtue of the national debt. The higher the national debt, the greater the impact on income inequality. In addition, the higher the debt, the higher the taxes needed to finance it, other things being equal. This may create some work disincentives and hence reduce real GNP—and the downward flexibility of federal spending is clearly reduced, since interest on the national debt is an obligatory, contractual payment.

The national debt is fairly widely distributed in the United States and for many groups constitutes an important proportion of their individual wealth. It is, indeed, a safe, liquid, and convenient form in which to keep one's assets—an investment which returns a safe, though modest, yield. As such, it may serve to raise the proportion of consumption out of current income.

All of these effects of the national debt (except those on income distribution) have the tendency to raise total spending above the levels it would have reached without it. Whether that is good or bad depends on whether the economy "needs" stimulus or restraint. By itself, a high internally held national debt is neither fish nor fowl. In the current inflationary context, it is probably mildly disadvantageous—"mildly disadvantageous" because the relative importance of the national debt and interest payments thereon is small.

The total national debt of the United States in December 1979 was $845.1 billion or about 35% of nominal GNP. Gross interest paid in 1979 was approximately $53 billion or barely 2.2% of nominal GNP. Since about 36% of the national debt is held by government accounts and the Federal Reserve system, the *net* interest payments as a proportion of GNP is well below 2% per year. Thus, the quantitative importance of the above effects is very small. Indeed, most economists and some others view the national debt as a relatively trivial matter so long as it is largely internally held and so long as the economy continues to grow in real terms. At present, the national debt is not very burdensome. However, both of the above caveats began to change in the 1970s. The proportion of the U.S. national debt held by foreigners has risen, and the growth rate of the U.S. economy has slowed. While still not a matter to become unduly exercised about, the national debt may increase in relative importance if these trends continue. The "debt service" problem, so significant for many of the world's poor economies, may assume more than marginal importance in the future for the United States.

In the meantime, however, the mistaken belief that the national debt was a serious problem clearly inhibited sensible application of monetary and fiscal policies.

The Need and Ability to Predict

An activist fiscal policy requires at least reasonably accurate predictions. The federal budget is proposed by the president several months before the fiscal year to which it applies. Thus, economic forecasts need to be made at least a year and a half in advance. These forecasts must relate expected total spending (relative to the capacity of the economy to produce) to the situation anticipated with existing expenditure and tax programs. If it is expected that total spending will exceed the capacity to produce, inflationary pressures will result. On the other hand, if total spending is estimated to be less than the capacity to produce, unemployment will rise. The policy responses to these forecasts will dictate the need for either a contractionary or expansionary budget (i.e., a surplus or a deficit). When considered in the light of probable monetary policy, these forecasts dictate general changes in tax rates, expenditure levels, or both.

Note that two sets of predictions are necessary—one relating to total spending and the other to the capacity to produce. Both are difficult and uncertain. Many models of the economy exist that relate each of the components and subcomponents of aggregate demand $(C + I + G + X - M)$ to their major determinants in a series of equations usually numbering in the hundreds.[9] The advent of the computer has raised the level of sophistication of such models and has permitted the inclusion of many more variables and numerous feedback effects. All models, however, rely on the validity and stability of their empirically derived coefficients. If these vary, the estimates will be far from the mark. In addition, the role of expectations, so influential in determining household and business expenditure behavior, is very difficult to gauge or measure accurately.

It is little wonder that forecasts are frequently far from the mark. Indeed, during 1979, all of the major models estimated that the contraction would occur in that year. It did not. Nor did any model predict the speed of the decline in output and rise in the unemployment rate early in 1980. Thus, prediction, while necessary for sensible monetary and fiscal policy, remains an art despite our increased capability and knowledge of modeling the economy.

On the supply side, forecasts are equally shaky, since they involve productivity estimates that fluctuate sharply on a year-to-year basis. Nor do many of the econometric models include much in the way of supply-side responses to tax changes or other policy variables.[10] Policies to restrain aggregate demand may also reduce capacity—the tax disincentive argument—and hence not have much anti-inflationary impact. The role of incentives and expectations is difficult to measure or even model with much certainty.

Thus fiscal policy with its lead time of a year to a year and a half is indeed subject to forecasting errors that may be substantial. On the other hand, monetary policy can be changed rapidly if a mistake has been made. It is relatively quick to implement and quick to reverse.

These difficulties, along with others to be discussed below, have led some thoughtful observers to conclude that an activist fiscal policy requiring frequent changes in tax rates and public expenditures may create more instability than would otherwise exist. A regular "stop-go" approach may in fact be unsettling and ineffective over the long pull. We therefore have recommendations designed to fix certain targets and to stick with a policy designed to achieve them. This larger issue of rules versus discretion in monetary and fiscal policy becomes subsumed in the debate between the Keynesians and monetarists, of which more later.

But while the problems of prediction create difficulties, especially for fiscal policy, there are associated difficulties with respect to the various time lags.

Time Lags

There are three types of lags important for an effective activist monetary and fiscal policy. First is what may be called the "recognition" lag. At what point do certain economic indicators provide enough evidence that the economy is moving in such an undesirable direction that a policy shift is warranted? One month's bad inflation news may be a statistical fluke or a temporary aberration. If the news continues to be adverse for another month, does this warrant policy actions? How many consecutive months of bad news is required before initiating policy changes? The data are almost always revised several months later, so the policymaker has a difficult time in discerning significant and persistent changes that call for new initiatives to offset them.

Thus for many months during 1978, the Carter Administration adopted a policy of benign neglect in the face of sharp reductions in the foreign exchange value of the dollar. Only when it became evident that this was more than a temporary speculative binge did the President, on 1 November 1978, announce policy initiatives designed to stabilize the exchange value of the dollar. Different interpretations of the international monetary scene might well have produced earlier or later reactions. The severity of the recession, especially in the second quarter of 1980, raised immediate cries for a sharp tax reduction either to take effect in 1980 or 1981. Until the sharpness of the economic decline was more accurately assessed, many economists viewed a tax cut even in 1981 as premature if we were serious about making a major anti-inflationary effort. Others disagreed and urged immediate action to halt the downturn.

For policymakers, there is always a real question of how much longer to wait to see if the bad news continues or begins to "bottom out." As we now know, the bottoming out apparently occurred about mid-1980. But the uncertainty of this led to the above conflicts typical of the recognition lag.

A second lag involves the length of time required to "implement" a policy shift after deciding that one is needed. For fiscal policy, the implementation lag can be very long indeed. In the next section, I shall outline the difficulties encountered in achieving President Johnson's surcharge finally enacted in late 1967. The problem in the United States is that all tax changes have to be passed by the House of Representatives. The president has no discretionary power to alter tax rates without congressional approval. The, usually, powerful chairman of the House Ways and Means Committee can therefore "bargain" with any presidential request for a change in taxes. It often happens that a presidential request for tax rate changes is linked with "tax reform" by the chairman as a sort of quid pro quo. By the time the bargaining and the hearings are over, many months will have passed and the fiscal medicine may be too little or too much—but in any case too late.

Congress is likewise reluctant to approve tax *increases* but generally approves tax *decreases*. It is better politically to give something to some-one than to take it away. Thus, fiscal policy invariably errs on the side of excessive stimulus and inadequate restraint. This is a problem by itself, but in the present context, the need for congressional approval of tax changes, combined with congressional reluctance to approve tax in-creases, adds to the delay already noted in the recognition lag.

Similar problems emerge with an expenditure change. If it is decided for expansionary purposes that federal spending should rise, time is required to specify what programs, old or new, should expand. Even more time is required to convince a skeptical Congress that such pro-grams are the most desirable or even that fiscal stimulus is necessary. Still greater difficulties arise if expenditures are to be cut. To decide which programs to cut and by how much requires a lot of time to deter-mine with any sense of reasonableness. Every program has its congres-sional constituency who will resist reductions and prolong the debate.

Thus, the most serious weakness of fiscal policy is its often long imple-mentation lag and its one-sided proclivity to err in the anti-inflationary direction. "Budgetary restraint" is therefore more difficult to implement than "budgetary stimulus." However, this situation may be changing as the myth of the sanctity of a balanced federal budget, currently espoused by both Democrats and Republicans as a goal, seems to have been resur-rected in and of itself despite its logical absurdity. As of the end of 1980, however, the attempt to balance the budget does make economic sense. Much of the resurrection of the desirability of an annually balanced bud-get appears to be related to the policy mistakes of the past 20 years, as well as to the difficulties already noted and others to be outlined below. A certain disillusionment with activist fiscal policy has settled on the land.

On the other hand, monetary policy suffers far less from the implemen-tation lag than does fiscal policy. The Fed can respond to particular situations very rapidly and can reverse itself equally fast as it perceives that a change is required. Although there are somewhat more solid grounds for the monetarist position, certainly the time-lag differential between implementation of monetary and fiscal policies gives the nod to the monetarists.

The third lag—the impact lag—concerns the amount of time after the policy change has been implemented for its effects to be felt on the economy. Clearly, neither households nor businesses revise their expen-diture decisions immediately with every change in disposable income or in profit prospects caused by a tax or public expenditure change. Nor do savings and investment decisions respond rapidly to changes in the money supply and interest rates. There is always a certain "wait-and-see" attitude involved. Households can maintain consumption levels by reducing the rate of savings, as has occurred the last several years, or by increasing it in response to tax changes. Business responds to changing demands by accumulating or reducing inventories. There are, in short, various "cushions" that prevent policy changes from showing up immediately in aggregate expenditure changes.

In addition, inertia plays a major role. Households and businesses develop habits and routines that inhibit rapid responses to alterations in, say, disposable income or prospective profits. Consumption and investment expenditures depend on a variety of factors other than current disposable income and profit prospects, not the least of which are confidence and expectations. Thus any change in monetary or fiscal policies only influences but does not determine exactly the magnitudes of consumption and investment outlays, and then only after a lag of uncertain duration and in particular patterns over time. Estimates of the impact lag range from three months (one quarter), to almost two years, and all such estimates vary with particular circumstances. This unpredictability poses a real dilemma for policymakers and may induce precipitate reactions in the mistaken belief that past actions were either not strong enough or too strong.

Monetary and fiscal policy changes only create the *conditions* for an expansion or contraction of aggregate expenditures. Individuals and businesses are free to respond to such changed conditions in any way they see fit. While human behavior in the aggregate is more predictable (as a noted philosopher once put it, "the individual man is an insoluble puzzle, man in the aggregate is a mathematical certainty"—a proposition that makes insurance companies profitable), nonetheless the precise relationships and their associated time lags are not known with much precision.

Choice of Policy Instruments

Changes in taxes, public spending, transfer payments, the money supply, and the rate of interest can each, in principle, influence the level of total spending. The economy may be stimulated by a tax reduction or an increase in federal expenditures or some combination of both. Reliance on a tax reduction in 1964 rather than on an expenditure increase was based on two assumptions—first, that the capital stock of the United

States appeared in need of some upgrading, which suggested the need for some special stimulus to private investment, and, second, that President Kennedy's difficulties with Congress were such that expanded federal programs would have been difficult to enact. The choice was then made to hold the line on spending and to reduce taxes.

Such choices are, however, not easy to make. Nor can they be made on the basis of pure objectivity. It is here that political judgment concerning feasibility, rather than economic analysis, comes into play. Yet there are obvious side effects on the economy of such choices. For example, an activist fiscal policy that relied on tax reductions rather than spending changes would tend to maintain or decrease slightly the relative share of federal spending in GNP, whereas an activist policy using public spending but maintaining tax rates would have the opposite impact.

More important is the relative weight to be accorded monetary policy vis-à-vis fiscal policy. An activist monetary policy in the face of a passive fiscal policy will, for example, put the brunt of the efforts to contain inflation on those industries most heavily influenced by credit availability and interest rates, namely housing and automobiles and other large durable goods. The recession of 1980 was led by sharp declines in home construction and automobile production in response to the very heavy reliance on a tight money policy and relative fiscal passivity. Likewise, money markets (especially in bonds) and thrift institutions like savings and loan associations suffer unduly when prime reliance is placed on monetary restraint. Indeed, in Chile recently, the thrift industry has almost been wiped out by such a one-sided attack on inflation. The U.S. savings and loan industry is having its worst year in history.

Such differential impacts are, of course, unintended. Yet the differential sensitivity of specific industries to monetary conditions inevitably subjects some to severe hardship compared to others when monetary policy is the main or only instrument applied in an activist manner. In this sense, fiscal policy is more widely diffused when tax rates are changed, and hence it is "fairer" by some criteria.

However, it is more difficult in the United States to coordinate monetary and fiscal policy closely because the Fed, whose responsibility lies in the monetary area, is relatively "independent" of the Administration and Congress. If the Fed's perception of the amount of stimulus or contraction that is needed differs from that of the Treasury and the President's economic advisors, the Fed can act to counter the fiscal policy impacts of the latter. Indeed, it has often done so, as illustrated in the following

section. This situation also raises the issue of accountability when monetary and fiscal policies work at cross purposes. Which agency is to blame
if the economic results are undesirable? How can mistakes be prevented
under such circumstances, especially if a broad consensus cannot be
reached about the magnitude of the stimulus or contraction required and
the relative influence to be played by monetary and fiscal policy? More
than once in the past 20 years, the Chairman of the Board of Governors
of the Fed has "broken" with the Administration over such questions,
and more than once has the Fed choked off an expansion prior to
achieving the goal of reasonably full employment. Conversely, as already
noted, fiscal policy invariably errs in the opposite direction.

Consistency among Macroeconomic Objectives

It may not be possible to achieve all of the macroeconomic goals simul-
taneously. Such goals are: full employment, stable prices, rapid growth,
and balance of payments equilibrium. Yet these goals are not only difficult to measure accurately, they may be partially inconsistent as well.
Measurement problems concerning the first two have already been noted.
If we are unsure of what constitutes full employment (i.e., what is the
full-employment unemployment rate—4%, 6%, or more?) or of what
constitutes "stable" prices (i.e., what rate of change of which index of
prices "really" means price stability?), policy making must take place in
a rather fuzzy context. While a policy consensus that unemployment
rates "close to" say 5% and a rate of change of most price indexes of the
same magnitude constitutes reasonable performance, there is much uncertainty. After all, every one percent change in the unemployment rate
affects over one million workers in the United States—at present with a
labor force of over 100 million. Every one percent change in the general
rate of inflation likewise affects the real incomes and real value of monetary assets of virtually everyone.

Rapid economic growth is likewise subject to empirical ambiguity.
What real rate of rise of GNP is the economy capable of sustaining over
the longer pull? Is it the 10%-plus rate long experienced by the Japanese
economy or the 4–5% rate achieved by the U.S. economy in the past or
something in between? Should it be measured on a per capita basis or in
terms of the aggregate itself? Recent fears or beliefs that future real
growth of the U.S. economy may be around $1\frac{1}{2}$–$2\frac{1}{2}$%, less than half our
previous experience, are grounded in assumptions regarding the oil and
energy situation and views on the future course of U.S. productivity,

both of which may be unduly pessimistic. Estimates of U.S. growth capacity vary widely.

Nor is the situation concerning the balance of payments any more certain in a quantitative sense. What level of the U.S. payments deficit is consistent with a relatively stable value of the dollar vis-à-vis other currencies? Much depends on other peoples' willingness to hold the vast number of dollars regularly released to the world economy through U.S. payments deficits. This in turn partly reflects foreign perceptions of our ability to contain domestic inflation and resume steady economic growth. Thus the meaning to be attached to our macroeconomic objectives is subject to a substantial amount of statistical uncertainty.

But more important are the potential inconsistencies among them. For example, some (unknown) degree of price inflation may be required to stimulate rapid growth. Given a lagging adjustment of costs behind prices, mild inflation may stimulate profits and increase incentives to produce, so many people believe. The Brazilian economy with rates of inflation up to 100% per year nevertheless was able to grow in real terms at almost 11%. "Growth through inflation" became a popular phrase to characterize the Brazilian situation.

However, domestic inflation adversely affects the balance of trade (imports become relatively cheaper, exports relatively more expensive) and thus conflicts with the goal of balance of payments equilibrium.

We have already noted the alleged "trade-off" between inflation and unemployment under the label of "the Phillips curve." To the extent such trade-offs among the macroeconomic variables exist, the policymaker is faced with a real dilemma. Which of the desirable goals to emphasize then becomes an object of policy. How much to pursue one goal at the expense of others is not amenable to precise calculation. Nor is it clear at what point, say, inflation becomes inconsistent with further growth or the achievement of even reasonably full employment. Indeed, there is more than a lurking suspicion that many of the alleged trade-offs do not even exist as noted in our digression on the Phillips curve.

HOW DID WE GET INTO THIS MESS?

The foregoing catalog of difficulties of implementing sensible monetary and fiscal policies suggests that from time to time mistakes, often serious ones, will be made under a policy of activism. To shed some light on our current predicament—especially with respect to inflation—I shall

outline here some of the major economic and other events that have
occurred since the early 1960s.

The Years Prior to 1965

It will be recalled that Mr. Kennedy was elected in 1960 in the midst
of a sluggish economy—the later years of the Eisenhower Administration
had been characterized as years of "high level, creeping stagnation." The
unemployment rate averaged 6.8% throughout 1958, remained high during 1959 at 5.5%, and rose to over 6.5% in the last quarter of 1960. The
inflation rate increased by less than 3% in 1958 by all measures and declined even further during 1959 in terms of the CPI and WPI (now
referred to as the Producer Price Index). Indeed, the latter even became
negative in 1959 (see table 3.1). So Kennedy's main economic problem
was how to stimulate the system. He selected as key economic advisers
pure, unadulterated Keynesians who thought they knew precisely how
to control aggregate demand and could achieve full employment, stable
prices, and steady growth concurrently.

The most dramatic *economic* event, after educating Mr. Kennedy along
Keynesian lines, was the tax cut of 1964 implemented by the Johnson
Administration. The rationale for the tax cut came straight out of the
economics textbooks—and it worked almost precisely as anticipated. We
reached full employment by late 1965, without much of a price rise. The
CPI rose only 6½% over the period 1960–1965 and the WPI only 1.8%,
a record no other industrial nation was able to match. Productivity rose
rapidly and unit labor costs in manufacturing actually fell slightly. The
real rate of growth rose from 2¼% for the period 1953–1960 to 4½%
for 1960–1965.

This tremendous success flowing from deliberate policy actions led
economists and others to believe that we had finally learned how to control aggregate demand and could keep it growing at a rate consistent
with the ever-growing capacity of the system. Thus, it was believed we
could have high employment, stable prices, and rapid growth. Recessions,
inflation, etc., were things of the past *if* we used monetary and fiscal policy intelligently. This was the "New Economics." Economists became a
little brash and boastful. This was the time when certain anti-Keynesians
proclaimed that "We're all Keynesians now." There were still nagging
questions about whether the policies would work as well to *restrain* aggregate demand by tight money, higher taxes, lower public spending,
etc., but those were brushed aside in the euphoria following the great

success. However, the crucial test emerged more rapidly than anyone had imagined.

Trouble Brewing

Though 1965 looked good, by the year's end there were signs of excessive spending and defense expenditures were already scheduled to rise even more as the Indochina war began to escalate. In the fourth quarter of 1965, defense expenditures rose to almost $53 billion (annual rate) compared with $48.6 billion in the first quarter. The rate of increase in prices also rose.

In its Annual Report for 1966, the Council stated:

> With another large advance in total production ahead, defense needs will be met while consumer living standards again improve strongly and the capital stock is further enlarged. Indeed the *increase* in output available for civilian uses this year is expected to be one of the largest in our history. . . . Progress will continue in building the Great Society. . . . [But], rising defense requirements clearly complicate the task of economic policy. The stimulative fiscal policies of recent years have achieved their mission. . . . The same logic that called for fiscal stimuli when demand was weak now argues for a degree of restraint to assure that the pace of the economy remains within safe speed limits. Measures to moderate the growth of private purchasing power are needed to offset, in part, the expansionary influence of rising defense outlays if intensified price and wage pressures are to be avoided. . . . Fiscal policy stands ready to meet any changing needs and unanticipated developments, and will look to assistance from monetary policy in maintaining flexibility.[11]

The year 1966 proved to be the critical one. With an already buoyant economy close to capacity, defense spending rose even more rapidly in 1966 than before. As Weidenbaum put it later:

> *The most rapid period of expansion in military contracts to private industry occurred in 1966; so did the most rapid rate of price inflation in recent years.* But that was the period when . . . the Administration's economists were still congratulating themselves on the success of the 1964 tax cut and little need was felt, at least officially, for greater fiscal restraint. . . . The official budget and economic reports were very slow to pick up the expansionary impact of the Vietnam buildup. . . . *The net result is that the Federal Government, though apparently following a non-inflationary economic policy in 1966, was actually a major source of inflationary pressure in the American economy during that time.*[12]

But equally disastrous was the failure to gauge the full impact of the defense buildup. The January 1966, estimates of defense expenditures for fiscal 1967 was short by about $10 billion—this meant that expenditure forecasts for fiscal '67 were understated by about $25 billion—hence, no one was much worried about inflation.

Why the mistake? Four reasons are usually advanced:

1. Technical peculiarities arose in the way defense expenditures enter national income accounts. The impact of defense expenditures for goods produced under contract occurs as the work on the project is being done. Often, progress payments are made to defense contracts. Yet in the national accounts, purchases are recorded mainly on a delivery basis. In a period of rapid military buildup, increased defense production is recorded in the national accounts initially as an increase in private inventories and only later as defense purchases. Estimates, including an adjustment along these lines for late 1965, indicate that defense spending increased by almost $6 billion while the official national accounts data indicated only $3½ billion.[13]

2. Combat operations in Vietnam were not concluded by the end of the fiscal year as was implicit in the projections.

3. The Vietnam buildup was more rapid, and hostilities more intense, than expected.

4. A breakdown in communications developed between the Pentagon and the Bureau of the Budget.

Whatever the real reason, few people knew what the actual situation was; hence there was less concern about the need for contractionary policies than reality dictated. In addition, Mr. Johnson felt a strong commitment to push forward on domestic legislation for his Great Society program. Thus, the continuation of rising defense and nondefense spending pushed federal expenditures up from $118 billion in 1964 to $164 billion in 1967—as a percent of GNP they rose from 18.6% in 1964 to 20.6% in 1967.

The situation in 1966 clearly called for a tax increase—although appearances diluted its apparent urgency. Furthermore, Mr. Johnson did not believe that a general tax increase would pass the Congress and did not propose one.[14]

Adding fuel to the inflationary fires was a major investment boom, stimulated earlier by the tax decrease. As the CEA put it,

> the defense buildup ... reinforced the previously planned fiscal stimuli. . . . The expansion of defense spending contributed to a significant change in the climate of opinion. The Vietnam buildup virtually assured American businessmen that no economic reverse would occur in the near future.[15]

And so politics, delayed recognition of the impact of defense commitments and their underestimate, and large expenditure increases to support President Johnson's "Great Society" led to a failure to attack inflation early. This failure produced serious consequences later, as we shall see.

Now, this is not as black as it may seem—there were important issues to be resolved *even if* the inflationary pressures were accurately foreseen.

> The main issue arose from the need—since unemployment had been brought down to its interim goal of 4%—to make the critical value choice between possible inflation and distortion on the one hand, and more employment on the other. If unemployment were allowed to fall to 3%, we would extend employment opportunities . . . to the unskilled, the nonwhite, the very young and the very old in the work force.[16]

In any event, vigorous restrictive fiscal actions were not forthcoming. In the meantime, however, the Fed, responding to increasing demands for credit, openly broke with the Johnson Administration in December 1965, by raising the discount rate and slowing the growth of the money supply. This raised interest rates dramatically and reduced the flow of savings to savings and loan associations; as a consequence, housing starts fell sharply (by over 20%) during 1966.

Fiscal Sanity: 1967–68

The investment boom ended, a massive inventory adjustment ensued, and with continued declines in homebuilding, GNP stabilized for the first six months of 1967. Although consumer prices continued to rise, there was some slackening in inflationary indicators. Forecasts in January of '67 anticipated a resurgence of total spending by mid-year. On the basis of these forecasts, President Johnson requested a temporary 6% surcharge on personal and corporation tax receipts, effective July 1. The nation seemed to have had a second chance to get back on the noninflationary, full-employment growth path.

But Congress delayed action, wanting both expenditure reduction *and* tax reform. In the meantime, the recovery was stronger than anticipated —President Johnson requested a surcharge of 10% on August 3. The Fed, however, began to expand the money supply at a faster rate, anticipating a tax increase.

The tax bill was not passed and signed until 28 June 1968, a full year and a half beyond the time when fiscal restraint, already belatedly recognized, was needed. The President also lopped off $6 billion in expenditure requests from his January budget.[17]

Fearing "overkill," the Fed eased monetary conditions. However, consumers kept on spending at high rates, and investment rose more than expected. Thus, inflation worsened. During 1969 the CPI rose by 5.4%—a new high, at least since the Korean-bred inflation of 1951. In the meantime there were urban riots, campus uprisings, and a souring, contentious mood throughout the country associated with the Vietnam war.

A New President

In January 1969, President Nixon replaced Mr. Johnson. The crucial economic problem was inflation (unemployment was below 4%)—just the opposite economic situation that Mr. Kennedy had faced eight years before. Then began the "Game Plan." Essentially, the Game Plan was to exercise fiscal and monetary restraint to decelerate the rate of total spending and thus create enough excess capacity to induce price reductions and moderate wage demands.

However, both the price level continued to rise more rapidly than desirable and the unemployment rate increased faster than anticipated. The annual growth of GNP slowed to 6.5% in 1969 from over 9% the preceding year (fourth quarter 1967 to fourth quarter 1968). In the fourth quarter of 1969, real GNP was actually below its level in the third quarter—but prices kept rising at unacceptable rates while unemployment remained well below 4% throughout the year.

The plan for 1970 was to allow considerable slack during the first half of the year, with a stimulus being provided during the second half to prevent unemployment from rising too much. However, real output actually fell in 1970, while prices rose at 5.9%. And unemployment rose to 4.9% for the year as a whole, reaching 6% in December 1970. Wage increases were being negotiated on the basis of continuing inflationary expectations, even though de-escalation in Vietnam and a real hold down in federal expenditures occurred.

By August 1971, with another election approaching, it became clear that the Game Plan wasn't working—unemployment had risen to 6.1% and the CPI, while having declined in its rate of increase since June, was still rising at unacceptable rates. Then came the pressure on the dollar during the second week of August 1971, and the dramatic rise in the balance of trade and payments deficit. For the first time since well before World War II, the United States imported more than it exported in goods and services. The balance of merchandise trade shifted from a

$289 million surplus to deficits of over $1 billion which dramatically signified the end of an era in international economic relationships—deficits have occurred regularly ever since, and we have had continuing instability in the international monetary system. The relative failure of the Game Plan on top of this bad news led to the sudden and dramatic announcement of the New Economic Policy (NEP).

The NEP began with what was referred to as Phase I (15 August 1971). It was ostensibly a short-run shock designed to reduce the rate of price increase, expand employment, and positively influence the balance of trade. The NEP consisted of a 90-day freeze on wages, prices, and rents intended to break the inflation psychology; it repealed the 7% excise tax, increased personal income tax exemptions, and provided an investment tax credit; it imposed an import surcharge; and it raised the U.S. official price of gold from $35 to $38 per ounce (an 8½% devaluation) and abandoned the gold standard.

What were the effects of the NEP? The rate of price increases *during* the freeze were below the immediate prefreeze periods. Most of the indexes were decreasing, anyway, prior to the freeze, so how much the freeze helped is a moot point. The unemployment rate was virtually unchanged—real output increased sharply in the fourth quarter of 1971 and was over 5% higher than the fourth quarter of 1970. The merchandise balance of trade continued to worsen, and the total balance on goods and services turned sharply negative during the fourth quarter for the first time in history.

Phase II was announced 7 October to become effective 14 November 1971. It established a structure of wage-price controls and an implementing set of organizations, commissions, and boards—the Pay Board, for example, set a standard for permissible pay increases of 5½% per year.

The Price Commission did not permit price increases for individual firms if the firm's profit margin (as a percent of sales) exceeded the average profit margin of the best two of the three years preceding 15 August 1971. All price increases were to be submitted in advance by large firms (those with sales over $100 million) for approval and had to be cost justified. Agriculture was exempt.

Real output rose 6½% in 1972 over 1971, and the GNP deflator rose by 4.1%, while the CPI rose by only 3.3%. Unemployment fell from 6% in December 1971, to 5% in January 1973, in response to further tax reductions and general monetary ease. The economy was in the midst of a substantial boom. Unit labor costs declined as labor productivity recorded substantial gains; profits rebounded. It appeared as though the economy had gotten close to a full employment, noninflationary economy once again.

But there were danger signals. The WPI rose in December by the largest monthly rate in over 20 years because of an even sharper rise in agricultural prices. This increase brought the December index to a level 6.5% higher than 12 months earlier; this augured ill for the future, especially since the rate of increase rose to a 9.6% annual rate from September to December.

The foreign trade balance continued in deficit and for the year as a whole was −$4.2 billion, contrasted with "traditional" surpluses of +$4 to $6 billion in earlier years.

However, Mr. Nixon's overwhelming reelection victory in November 1972, his foreign policy initiatives and the Paris negotiations, along with the real economic boom, led to a certain predisposition to downplay the significance of the WPI increases. After all, one could blame these on the always volatile and uncertain agricultural sector. Furthermore, there were other things to worry about late in 1972—the environment, the energy "crisis," and so on. Campus unrest was over; blacks were apparently making real progress; urban riots had ceased; the real problems appeared to lie in the future.

Phase III was announced in January 1973, about the time the Paris Accords with the North Vietnamese were signed. The rationale for Phase III reflected a certain amount of euphoria—even though recognizing the seriousness of the sharp rise in food prices. It was believed in January of that year that it was desirable to "moderate the degree of detailed supervision and mandatory enforcement in the system in order to preserve the self-restraint which has been the essence of the program."

Accordingly, Phase III was initiated—the goal was to get the rate of inflation down to 2½% or below by the end of 1973. The price and wage standards of Phase II remained intact, but compliance was to be voluntary. The organizational structure of the controls was by and large dismantled, although authority remained in the Cost-of-Living Council to set ceilings on specific prices or wages and to monitor industrial performance.

Mandatory controls remained on food processing and distribution, medical care, the construction industry, interest and dividends. Special actions were also taken to expand food supplies. Rent controls were terminated.

As the Council put it, "the essence of Phase III is that the government retains the enforcement ability and authority necessary to the Nation's anti-inflation objective while leaving the private sector the maximum possible freedom to pursue productivity, efficiency, and collective bargaining,"[18]—the "club in the closet" approach.

Events during 1973

This year turned out to be critical, in some senses more significant than 1966, when serious overexpansionary forces associated with the Indochina wars led to excess demand inflation. This time, the economy was subjected to a series of supply-side shocks, while rational policy was largely immobilized by Watergate and the 1972 election promises by both candidates (McGovern and Nixon) *not* to raise taxes.

Largely in response to poor crops throughout the world and the Soviet Union's purchase of 19,000,000 tons of U.S. grains in the summer of 1972, wheat prices tripled in the 12 months ending August 1973, and prices for corn and soybeans more than doubled. The impact on the United States was dramatic. Food prices from December 1972, to December 1973, rose by more than 20%, leading to a doubling of the rate of growth of the CPI and almost tripling the rate of growth of the (then) wholesale price index compared with relatively inflationless 1972. The agricultural price explosion thus started early in 1973 after accelerating in late 1972.

As economic policy was reacting to these events with a new wage-price freeze (June 13–August 12), a new set of Phase IV Controls and modifications of earlier rules, tight monetary policy (which almost doubled the prime interest rate), and a slowdown in federal spending despite prior authorizations, a second supply-side shock occurred. On 6 October 1973, Egypt and Syria invaded Israel setting off the so-called Yom Kippur War, the results of which induced a hitherto harmless cartel (OPEC) to exploit to the hilt the "oil weapon." Ignoring the oil companies, on 17 October the cartel announced a price increase for its product of almost 70% (from $3.00 to $5.11 per barrel of Saudi Arabian light crude). This action was supported by an oil embargo against the United States and the Netherlands, both active supporters of Israel, and production cutbacks. By January 1974, the price was further raised to $11.65 per barrel.[19]

Earlier in the year, the foreign trade balance deteriorated, and in response the dollar was devalued again in February by 10%. Many currencies were floated. The spectre of sharp U.S. inflation led to considerable international monetary disarray. Gold prices rose to the then unbelievable price of $200 per ounce (it reached a high of over $800) as holders of depreciating dollars sought to get rid of them. The devaluation, of course, raised the price of imports generally and thus contributed further to domestic inflation.

Inflation was clearly out of control. Real output (GNP), however, rose sharply (by 5.5%) for the year as a whole, and the unemployment rate dropped below 5%. The discomfort index, however, averaged over 11% for the first time since 1951—the worst macro performance in over 20 years. The policy responses were essentially "more-of-the-same"—export embargoes, import controls, and other elements noted above.

Even the Indochina "accords" turned sour. The war had not ended and U.S. withdrawal was imminent. The events of 1973 spilled over into the following year and precipitated the worst recession since 1929–33.

The Worst Recession since the Great Depression (1974–75)

The high and rising inflationary rates in 1974 pushed the CPI up by 11% for the year as a whole. The increase in the Producer Price Index was higher by almost half again as much. The prime interest rate rose to over 10% in response both to the accelerating inflation rate and a tightening monetary policy. New housing starts and automobile production dropped sharply (shades of 1980!). Real GNP dropped by 1.4% from the previous year and continued to slide during the first half of 1975, leading to a further annual decline of 1.3%.[20] The unemployment rate increased sharply, reaching over 9% by mid-1975.

The combination of forces generated in 1972 and exacerbated in 1973 had drained the purchasing power of households. Inflation had also pushed up incomes and put people into higher income tax brackets (tax bracket creep), further limiting disposable income of households. "Paper" profits of corporations using the "first-in, first-out" method of inventory accounting likewise raised corporate taxes. These developments—combined with world monetary instability, high interest rates, and enormous uncertainty—caused a sharp reduction in investment spending. The continuing monetary and fiscal restraint further exacerbated the impact on total spending.

In the meantime, Watergate had taken its toll and President Nixon resigned in August 1974. Suddenly, President Ford had some difficult decisions to make regarding economic policy. Inflation was then continuing at an accelerating rate. Rates exceeding 1% *per month* (CPI) were regularly recorded through August and September. Even higher rates were recorded for the Producers' Price Index, making annual averages of well over 12%. "Double-digit" inflation, like Spiro Agnew, became a household word. President Ford thereupon pronounced that inflation was "public enemy number one." The unemployment rate was not then exceptionally high (less than 6%) and showed no signs of increase. Phase IV was allowed to die an ignominious death and was replaced with a Council on Wage and Price Stability with no powers other than the monitoring of price increases and persuasion. The experiment in price controls evaporated "not with a bang but with a whimper," as T. S. Eliot put it in another context. Although real output had decreased sharply in the first quarter of 1974, employers appeared reluctant to lay off workers, possibly in anticipation of an early turnaround.

However, the full extent of the contractionary forces appeared later, about two months after the assertion that inflation was public enemy number one. The President, in a startling turnabout, then proposed a massive tax reduction, which he got in January 1975.

The deficit in the federal budget mushroomed from less than $5 billion for fiscal year 1974 to over $45 billion in fiscal 1975. Fiscal stimulus to revive a sharply contracting economy was in place. Yet the Fed, fighting the ongoing inflation, maintained a relatively restrictive policy fearing excessive stimulus. Interest rates, though lower, remained relatively high, exacerbated by the possibility that New York City would declare bankruptcy and the continuing anxiety over inflation.

But the fiscal medicine appeared to work. Real output ceased to fall by the second quarter of 1975 and, in fact, turned up. Employment, however, lagged and the unemployment rate reached a post–World War II record high in May 1975, of 9.2%. Price indexes began to decrease from their earlier double-digit rates, and for 1975 as a whole the CPI averaged 9.1%—still incredibly high by historical standards (see table 3.1). For the year as a whole, the discomfort index reached a record 17.6%—a combination of an annual average unemployment rate of 8.5% and in inflation rate (CPI) of 9.1%. Clearly, as the then chairman of the Fed put it, the economy was not performing the way it should.

Economic Recovery and Jimmy Carter

The recovery, however, proceeded smoothly. Real GNP for 1976 recorded a healthy 5.9% gain. The rate of inflation fell by all indexes but remained positive and substantial by all past experience. The unemployment rate fell steadily during the year and averaged 7.7%. President Carter took office in January 1977, and announced an economic program of "caution." The overall strategy was to keep the momentum of overall real growth going and to strive for "full employment" by the early 1980s, in the meantime hoping to slow the real growth rate to its presumed long-term sustainable level (then believed to be 3–4% per year) and to moderate inflationary pressures.

In a series of policy statements and actions over the ensuing years, President Carter sought to respond to the ever-growing inflationary forces, not unlike the sequences of Phases, Freezes, and Fizzles of President Nixon, but with constant reassurance that wage-price *controls* would not be imposed. Indeed, the very prospect of wage-price controls induced labor and business to push up prices as fast as they could to avoid being caught with their prices down. Anticipated controls are counterproductive, especially after a succession of them in an on-again, off-again fashion, which failed to stem the inflationary tide earlier.

Modest but permanent tax reductions were enacted during 1976 and 1978, mainly to sustain the recovery and partially to compensate for the impact on taxes of rising nominal incomes and higher social security taxes. Real GNP grew briskly during 1976, and the inflation rate dropped sharply. However, on an annual basis since 1976, real output growth declined steadily to barely 2.3% during 1979, while the inflation rate regularly increased by all indexes, with double-digit rates occurring in 1979 for both the CPI and PPI. At the same time, the unemployment rate steadily declined from the 8.5% level during the last year of the recession to 5.8% in 1979.

The recurrence of domestic inflation induced sharp declines in the foreign exchange value of the dollar. Events in Iran led to a renewal of large oil price increases and the U.S. balance of payments turned sharply negative in 1977 and 1978. Fiscal and monetary restraint led to rapidly rising interest rates and a decline in real output growth.

The stock market plunged, gold prices soared, and voluntary wage-price guidelines (not controls) were ceremoniously announced in October 1978, to be "enforced" by an enlarged Council on Wage and Price Stability under the vigorous leadership of Alfred E. Kahn.

Inflation once more seemed out of control. The only cure appeared to be a heavy dose of monetary and fiscal restraint, overt pressures on individual firms and labor to stay within the wage-price guidelines, and creation of enough slack in the system to exert downward pressure on the price level. However, inflationary pressures were being generated by both supply-side forces as well as demand. Difficulty in controlling the latter, never easy at best, and marginal ability to influence the former (since much of the supply-side forces originated outside the nation), did not augur well for the deteriorating economic situation. The attack on inflation, deemed mandatory by most observers (public enemy number one and all that), appeared to require even stronger measures. Thus the U.S. economy was widely believed to be heading for another recession during 1979, both through the processes of sharply higher energy prices (which reduced real disposable income of households and business profit prospects) and higher interest rates and through deliberate monetary and fiscal restraint. It looked like a partial replay of the Nixon Administration's ill-fated game plan of the early 1970s.

But the long-heralded recession did not occur during 1979. Almost all the forecasts were wrong, at least as to the timing of the recession and its magnitude when it did occur. To be sure, real GNP did decline during the second quarter of 1979, thereby heralding the onset of a recession— often defined as two successive quarters of negative growth. But expansionary forces continued strong, especially consumer spending—fueled by a sharp reduction in the household savings rate, which plunged to a low of 3.5% during the last quarter of 1979—as well as a willingness to borrow to maintain expenditure levels. Business inventories were not out of line; consumer spending therefore was more or less rapidly translated into output increases, and the unemployment rate stayed below 6% for the year as a whole.

But inflation rates remained at the double-digit level month after month. The voluntary wage-price guidelines seemed to be having little effect. Fiscal policy had already turned sharply restrictive, but without much apparent impact on inflation. The Council of Economic Advisors attributed this to the "huge oil price increases" during 1979 and the failure of inflation expectations to subside.[21] Oil prices indeed more than doubled from about $13 per barrel in December 1978 to over $28 per barrel by January 1980, and evidently price expectations failed to shift downwards.

As a result, monetary policy by the last quarter of 1979 turned sharply restrictive in an attempt to allay the burgeoning inflationary forces. The Fed not only raised the discount rate to a (then) record 12% but on 8 October 1979 announced a major shift in the way monetary policy was to be implemented. Henceforth, the primary target was to be the containment of growth of the money supply within a relatively low range (around 4% per year), letting interest rates bear the brunt of the adjustments. Additional reserve requirements were also imposed, thereby limiting new borrowing. As a result, interest rates shot up rapidly, reaching over 19% (prime rate) by March 1980 and 20% for several weeks in April 1980—an unprecendented rise.

Consumers and businesses alike responded, though with something of a lag. Although real output rose during the first quarter of 1980, the demand for housing and automobiles dropped sharply. Automobile sales plummeted some 40%, and housing starts, already down in November and December of 1979, fell even more sharply—from a September 1979 annual rate of over 1.8 million to a May 1980 estimate of barely 0.9 million. The spread effects of such sharp reductions in two important industries appeared in successive increases in the unemployment rate in April and May of over 800,000 workers to 7.8% in May. June 1980 unemployment stayed almost at this level.

Yet the inflation rate as measured by the CPI soared to almost 18% during the first quarter evoking headlines of "obscene," "out of control," "banana republic," and the like. Policymakers, believing that something more was required as early as March 1980, responded with a package of credit controls, including restrictions on and higher costs for credit card use among other things. On top of an already weakening economy, this additional restraint contributed to the surges in unemployment of April and May. Real output declined sharply during the second quarter of 1980.

Then a surprising thing happened. Interest rates broke in June, and the CPI rate of growth dropped back to the 12–14% level. The medicine of March appeared at last to break inflation expectations, at least partly.

Cries of "We need a tax cut" began to be heard. The empty vision of a balanced 1981 federal budget began to fade as recession-induced deficits of almost record amounts were contemplated. The magnitude and speed of the contractionary forces, many deliberately put in place, were in no way anticipated.

The "recession" of 1980, however, ended abruptly by mid-year, and real growth of GNP ensued during the third and (especially) the fourth quarters. Mr. Reagan was elected with a decisive majority for reasons only partly economic. After all, the so-called recession was the mildest of the postwar contractions. The evidence to date suggests a sluggish recovery from a possibly nonexistent recession. But real output rose by more than 8% during the first quarter of 1981!

The burning economic question for the 1980s was how to restrain further inflationary forces without causing real output to drop and the unemployment rate to rise so sharply. Fighting inflation via unemployment and lost output may be effective, but how long does it take? What depths of contraction and heights of unemployment must the economy suffer? Are the costs worth the gains? Economists and others simply do not know with any certainty. Fine tuning the economy on a month-to-month or quarter-to-quarter basis is an idea whose time has long since gone. The Reagan years may provide more acceptable alternatives, but uncertainty reigns despite a certain amount of business euphoria.

Lessons from These Experiences

The role of government in stabilizing the U.S. economy has swung from the heady, almost euphoric days of the early to mid-1960s when anything seemed possible (Camelot and all that) to the gloomy, uncertain atmosphere of the mid to late 1970s when nothing seemed possible. Is this due to a succession of mistakes in aggregate demand management policies, bad luck, or more fundamental changes in the structure of a postindustrial society that renders demand management less effective than previously?

Certainly, many mistakes were made in the period between 1960 and 1980. Monetary and fiscal policies often worked at cross-purposes. Serious delays were made in recognizing inflationary pressures and even longer delays in responding to them through tax increases or spending restraint. Monetary policy has swung from excessive restraint to excessive ease.

Bad luck likewise predominated in the 1973 supply-side shocks and the 1979 sharp increases in oil prices. Similarly, structural shifts in the economy such as the changing age and sex composition of the labor force, the changing overall composition of output in favor of service industries, the decreasing downward flexibility of prices, the increasing sensitivity of the U.S. economy to world economic and even political events as discussed in chapter 3. I shall discuss many of these issues further in chapter 7, which deals with "cures" for inflation.

Yet there are some specific economic lessons that have, in fact, been learned. First, the trade-off between inflation and unemployment is more complex and serious than hitherto believed; indeed, there may not even be a trade-off. Second, this implies that the causes of inflation and unemployment go well beyond excesses or deficiencies of total spending, as the last chapter and this one seek to elaborate. Third, the ability to control the economy, even to control simply the level of nominal GNP, is seriously impeded by inadequate knowledge of time lags, the now perceived far more critical role of expectations, the increased difficulty of prediction of many key variables and their interrelations, the qualitative deficiencies of much of the data upon which policy and expectations are based (e.g., the CPI, the unemployment rate, GNP itself[22]) and aspects of our political institutions that impede even rational stabilization policies. Fourth, the foreign trade sector responds more slowly to changes in the value of the dollar than hitherto believed, although part of the data are clouded by oil price behavior. Fifth, it is widely believed that even sensibly administered, coordinated, and effectively carried out monetary and fiscal policies will not be enough to reduce significantly the inflation and unemployment rates to tolerable levels.

On this latter point, after a detailed empirical analysis, Otto Eckstein concludes that

> the fiscal and monetary policies which the government employs to manage aggregate demand must create a constructive environment in which inflation can be improved, but they cannot, by themselves, solve the problem. Aggressive demand management, aiming at unemployment rates averaging 6 percent or less every year, makes it impossible to have any other policy succeed. The inflation will simply become worse and worse—until the public despairs and forces politicians to adopt price controls. But even if demand management sets its gauges to achieve unemployment in the 6.5 to 7 percent area, the inflation problem is not solved. . . . (I)t is beyond the capacities of management to bring down inflation adequately.[23]

This is not as bleak as it sounds for there are a series of so-called supply-side and other measures that can be undertaken (see chapter 7) which, in combination with improved and steadier demand management, may be effective. However, no one can be sure, and the economic situation is likely to stay messy through 1985 because many of the supply-side measures, designed to raise productivity, will take an unknown amount of time to be effective.

OTHER GOVERNMENT POLICIES INFLUENCING INFLATION

The role of government in the inflationary process extends well beyond the sphere of managing total spending for the economy as a whole. Most of the following aspects of federal policy at the microeconomic level, all well-intentioned and often needed to some degree because of evidences of market failure, serve to raise business costs in one way or another, and/or to reduce business productive investments (which has a similar though longer range impact). They all, in short, reinforce downward wage-price rigidity already noted in chapter 3 and, with the rapid expansion of public efforts in some of these directions, put distinct and growing upward pressure on the entire cost structure. We turn now to an examination of some of these policies and activities.

Direct Economic Regulation

The federal government has long subjected specific industries to direct regulatory control involving rate or price fixing; entry, exit, or abandonment control; financial requirements and methods; and even specified accounting procedures. Transportation, electric utilities, communications, banking, the security exchanges, and other industries are subject to some or all of these restrictions. For each industry or set of industries, specific regulatory commissions have been established to "protect the public interest." The first such agency was the Interstate Commerce Commission (ICC), established in 1887 to prevent monopolistic exploitation and excessive price discrimination by the railroads.

Since the early to mid-1960s, attacks on these regulatory agencies, mainly by economists, have mounted as increasingly the costs of regulation, in all of its aspects, appeared drastically to exceed the benefits to society. Thus, for example, ICC refusal or reluctance to allow abandonment of lightly used rail track or service, forced freight rates higher on other traffic to offset the losses on unprofitable business. The Civil Aeronautics Board's refusal to permit rate or fare competition induced the airlines to compete on the basis of larger, faster aircraft, many seeking to arrive at key destinations at the same time. The resultant excess capacity in the airlines and congestion at airports raised unit costs of providing air service, which induced requests for higher general rate levels normally granted to ensure a "fair return" on asset values. The lack of rate competition also raised costs as the companies sought to improve the real or apparent quality of their services to lure traffic away from their rivals.

It is widely believed that economic regulation in general has stifled innovation, absorbed too much management talent in details of the regulatory process itself (thereby diverting concern away from operating efficiency), and imposed excessive compliance costs or restrictions on operations that raised production costs. Specific rate or price reductions proposed by more efficient rail, truck, or air carriers were frequently rejected or sharply modified due to protests of competing carriers, while general increases were normally granted. The imposition of excess capacity on the industries, combined with refusal to sanction price competition which would have increased use, raised average production costs. Many other similar allegations or findings were made. Indeed, these formed the basis for the so-called deregulation movement in transportation and communications—a movement to allow competitive forces to work and thus reduce the degree of downward price rigidity and provide incentives to raise productivity by virtue of the increased competition. Economic regulation of airlines, trucking, and railroads has sharply been reduced in the past two years.

Although the immediate results have often been to raise rates and fares—especially in the wake of sharp increases in fuel costs—in the long run the outcome should conform more to the competitive model.[24] Indeed, part of the rationale for regulatory reform was that it should positively contribute to a resolution of stagflation.

Indirect Economic Regulation

Contrary to the regulatory reform movement for direct, Commission, industry-specific regulation, new non-industry-specific regulations have burgeoned since 1960. Problems of pollution, discrimination, worker health and safety, consumer protection from hazardous drugs, materials and products have increasingly captured public attention. These external "bads"—often generated in the process of producing "goods"—represent a species of market failure in the sense that private firms do not directly bear the costs that pollution and these other evils impose on society. Indeed, pursuit of the profit motive would make such activities self-perpetuating—the market itself would not correct the hazards created by a rampant industrialization. Early in the 1960s, people like Ralph Nader and Rachel Carson began calling attention to unsafe vehicles and environmental degradation. Earlier still, issues of racial discrimination were taken up by the civil rights movement, discrimination against women by the women's liberation movement, and so on. The public became alarmed by race riots, the possibility of ecological disaster, and cancer-inducing substances that were regularly emitted into the environment.

Later, nuclear energy, once seen as a major alternative to energy dependence, came under attack. This was not only due to the possibility of more Three Mile Islands but, perhaps as important, to nuclear waste disposal (à la Love Canal) and transportation of radioactive substances, often through densely populated areas.

In the wake of growing concern, Congress responded with over 90 pieces of legislation to curb the side effects of otherwise productive activity and created a series of new commissions, agencies, and administrations to interpret and enforce the plethora of new laws. Thus we got, in addition to the Food and Drug Administration, which had long been established, the Environmental Protection Agency, the Equal Employment Opportunity Commission, the Occupational Safety and Health Administration, the Consumer Products Safety Commission and others, all designed to enforce laws that, while nobly establishing general goals, were deliciously vague as to precisely how to establish exact standards and enforce them.

Many of the new agencies—staffed by bright, eager, dedicated people—went to work with gusto. Standards were set, inspections made, court cases initiated, and fines imposed for noncompliance with essentially arbitrary but occasionally whimsical standards. In some cases, timetables were established for compliance that could not be met until new technology was developed.

As the vigor of some of the new agencies expanded, the costs of compliance with the new rules of the game became increasingly burdensome to businesses, nonprofit institutions (like universities), cities, and municipalities. Indeed, this was partly the intent. For example, products that pollute the atmosphere causing acid rain, respiratory diseases, and so on, were being produced in excessive amounts because the producers did not pay the full social costs. Imposition of such costs would, of course, raise the price of the products and discourage their use, at the same time providing producers with an incentive to avoid the new costs (in various forms) associated with polluting activities. Likewise, discrimination became expensive under the threat of expensive law suits and heavy fines, as many large enterprises discovered.

Rising costs and prices are therefore partly due to the activities of the new agencies. To the extent that such costs and prices merely internalize the negative externalities to the producers, they are socially beneficial in the sense that markets will function more efficiently and more correctly match demands with marginal social costs as well as provide incentives to find and utilize production processes with fewer social costs. But in many instances the changes in the rules of the game occasioned needless costs—or at least costs far in excess of any perceived benefits.[25] They therefore contributed needlessly to higher costs and prices. Similarly, they often jeopardized the internal efficiency of firms as many managers and chief executive officers found themselves spending more and more time in Washington protesting the latest ruling, or otherwise preparing legal defenses, rather than concerning themselves with better production techniques. Paperwork to prove compliance or attempts at compliance mounted. Environmental impact statements were required for many large new investments. Affirmative action plans had to be prepared. A typical *Wall Street Journal* headline screamed that EPA's "proposed new toxic rules may require 600,000 firms to keep files 5 to 30 years."[26] An audit of 48 large firms in 1977 found that the added total costs (including mandated investments) attributable to EPA, OSHA, and EEOC plus two others amounted to $2.6 billion—equivalent to 16% of the companies' net profits and 10% of their capital expenditures.[27] Extensive and elaborate testing of new drugs was increasingly required as medical research revealed more and more adverse side effects and serious potential health hazards from various types of drugs and emissions.

No one can fault the intent to improve the quality of health and the environment. Nor can one doubt that unrestricted economic growth was imposing increasing environmental problems, some potentially irreversible. But there is little doubt that the added costs[28] not only pushed up prices but also slowed the rate of investment and altered its direction in the form of, for example, antipollution equipment like scrubbers on smokestacks. Perhaps as much as 10% of new U.S. investment is designed to produce cleaner air and so forth, rather than goods and services. Since "cleaner air" is not a marketable product and hence its value does not appear in the GNP estimates, measured capital and labor productivity will decline. In a "'real" sense this is spurious, but it nevertheless reduces efficiency in the narrow sense by which we measure it. This, again, raises unit costs of the goods and services we actually do buy and sell.

The early failure to consider the total costs of compliance and weigh these against putative benefits—no easy task, to be sure—doubtless contributed not only to rising prices and wages but embedded new permanently higher rising levels in costs to firms, colleges, cities, and so on.

Price Support Programs

The federal government has elaborate price support programs for agriculture, milk producers, and others. The minimum wage laws are likewise a form of price support on which we have already commented. Such programs, designed to maintain farmers' and low income workers' incomes, are understandable—though not especially intelligent—responses to the volatility of agricultural prices and to prevent exploitation in one segment of the labor market. Regardless of their dubious merits, such policies and programs reinforce the downward rigidity of the wage and price structure and thus impede price declines when demand slackens even in an industry so potentially competitive as agriculture. New and invariably higher price supports for such products as wheat, corn, and soybeans are regularly announced[29] and contribute to the upward cost-price spiral (perhaps better described as the "ratchet" effect).

CONCLUSION

The existence of substantial downward price rigidity means that so long as the economy suffers from some degree of inherent instability or from frequent excesses of aggregate spending, the general price level will show a persistent tendency to rise over time. Cyclical expansions will be accompanied by price rises of varying magnitudes, but any subsequent contractions, however caused, will not be followed by overall price reductions—merely a reduction in the previous rate of inflation. Therefore all those factors that tend to strengthen this rigidity will accentuate the degree of secular rise in the price level.

The role of government in the process of inhibiting certain price reductions as well as raising costs is certainly far from minimal. Important as some of the cost enhancing and rigidifying measures are in other contexts, as noted above, their role in the inflation process cannot be denied.

To be sure, downward price rigidity does not *initiate* inflation, but it does make the attempts to offset inflationary forces, once begun, far more difficult and painful, since the brunt of contractionary forces will fall much more on output and employment than on prices. Anything that can be done to stimulate more price flexibility, within the constraints set by other goals, will contribute to our willingness and ability to pursue rational policies of monetary and fiscal restraint. Part—perhaps only a small part—of any long-run attack on inflation must therefore include a reconsideration of the public policies indicated in this chapter. To these I shall return in chapter 7.

Other Laws and Regulations Relevant to Downward Price Rigidity

Surprisingly enough, certain aspects of our antitrust (or procompetition) laws may in fact inhibit the very price competition that they are generally intended to preserve. Obviously, so-called fair-trade laws, whereby manufacturers are allowed to set *retail* prices for their products and to have such prices legally enforced, inhibit price competition. For many

years, following the passage of such laws in 1937, prices of many household items were maintained well above any reasonable estimate of their
competitive level. However, the rise of discount stores in the 1950s and
'60s served to undermine, at least partially, some of the worst effects.
In 1975, the federal government repealed these laws; they therefore no
longer operate as a barrier to price reductions or price competition at
the retail level.

The antidiscrimination amendment to the Clayton Act, the Robinson-
Patman Act of 1937, is believed to have inhibited price reductions—especially by large, dominant firms—since it required price reductions or
discounts to be cost-justified and available to all similarly situated buyers.
The intent was to stop predatory pricing, but it is difficult in practice
to distinguish between "predatory" and competitive pricing. At any rate,
the effects on overall price rigidity are probably slight.

Other aspects of the antitrust laws tend to have somewhat similar
effects. On the whole, however, such laws have had some beneficial impact and have probably retained a higher degree of price competition
and price flexibility than would have obtained in their absence. How
important they have been in this endeavor is a matter of considerable
debate. It is, however, better to have legal prohibitions against price
fixing arrangements, monopolization, "unfair" competition, and the like,
than to either sanction them or tolerate them. These prohibitions operate
in the interests of retaining a consumer sovereignty economy, efficient
resource allocation mechanisms, and a higher degree of price flexibility
than would exist without them.[30]

5 The Role of Money

INTRODUCTION

To the extent that the money supply is controlled by governments, this chapter is really an extension of the previous chapter. However, in the United States and several other countries, the control of the money supply has been vested in a more or less independent agency variously called the Bank of Canada, the Bank of England, or, in the United States, the Federal Reserve System (the Fed). The governing body of the Fed does not consist of elected officials but appointees of the administration for fourteen-year staggered terms in the U.S., specifically designed to give the Fed's governors independence from any administration. Since the Fed is a creation of the Congress (1913), Congress can change the basis of its authority at any time if the majority feels that the Fed is not performing its monetary role in a desirable fashion. Thus, though technically independent, the Fed always has its eye on Congressional sentiment. Yet remarkably few attempts have successfully curbed the Fed's independence or its aura of being above the political fray (in a sense that an elected administration could never be). This is one reason why fiscal policy implementation is so slow, while monetary policy changes require only a majority of a small governing body. In 1975, to be sure, Congressional concern over the course of monetary policy led to a House Concurrent Resolution requiring the Fed to report to Congress at quarterly intervals on the course of monetary policy and to provide an assessment of future desirable ranges of increase in the money supply and other monetary and credit aggregates. Essentially, this merely required the Fed, hitherto often close-mouthed about what it was attempting in any specific sense and why, to communicate more fully and to hear Congressional concerns. It still retains a high degree of independence, but now clothed in far less secrecy than in the past.[1]

However, the issue at hand is not so much whether the Fed is or even should be "independent" but, rather, how economic activity is affected by changes in the money supply that can be determined by specific and deliberate actions of the Fed. At the outset, we need to clarify two issues: What is meant by the money supply? and How can the Fed change the money supply?

WHAT IS THE MONEY SUPPLY?

Broadly speaking, money is anything that people are willing to accept in exchange for goods and services. Many things have served as money, from cattle (*pecus* in Latin, hence our word pecuniary) to cowrie shells to cigarettes (in POW camps) to gold, silver, copper, bronze, to instrinsically worthless pieces of paper issued by commercial or central banks. These things because of widespread acceptance have from time to time performed the functions of money, whose primary purpose is the facilitation of exchange in place of the clumsy barter system. So long as one knows that others will accept the money substance in exchange for real goods and services, he or she is willing to accept it in exchange for his or her real goods and services and debt repayment.

In modern economies, the inconveniences or excessive scarcity of many of these previously used monetary units have given rise to paper currencies or coins having little or no intrinsic value of their own. Demand deposits at banks are also money in this sense because they can quickly and cheaply be converted into coin and currency. Thus, a narrow contemporary definition of the money supply (designated M_1 or, more recently, M_{1A} in the United States) is coin and currency outside the banking system plus demand deposits in commercial banks. As time has gone on, however, the distinction between demand deposits and time or savings deposits at commercial banks has progressively blurred. There are also checkable deposits (such as NOW accounts) at thrift institutions and credit unions, and it has become increasingly easy and costless to withdraw coin and currency from savings accounts in thrift institutions, even though checks drawn in favor of third parties cannot be honored. Thus a broader definition of the money supply would involve these as well (often called M_2). A historical series from 1867 to 1960 is shown in figure 5.1. Line C in this figure coincides with a definition of money, including time and demand deposits at banks, but excludes deposits at savings and loan associations and credit unions. Note that the money supply, so defined, rose from some $1,314 million in 1867 to $206 billion in mid-1960, a 157-fold increase or an average annual compound rate of increase of about 5.5%.

The rise in the money supply has not been steady and over all it has

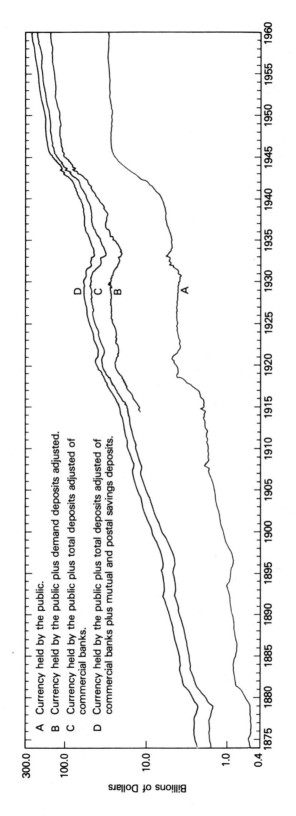

Fig. 5.1 Deposits and Currency, 1874–1960

Source: Milton Friedman and Anna J. Schwartz, *A Monetary History of the United States, 1867–1960* (Princeton: Princeton University Press, 1963), chart 1.

A Currency held by the public.
B Currency held by the public plus demand deposits adjusted.
C Currency held by the public plus total deposits adjusted of commercial banks.
D Currency held by the public plus total deposits adjusted of commercial banks plus mutual and postal savings deposits.

grown more rapidly than the current value of total output of the economy (nominal GNP or NNP)—except for the period from 1948 to 1960 when the money supply grew by about 2.9% per year compared with a growth of nominal output of 5% per year.[2]

Since 1960, the money supply estimates most consistent with the above (M_2) have risen from $217 billion as of December 1960,[3] to over $953 billion as of December 1979, an average rate of some 8% per year (see table 5.1). Nominal GNP also grew at a rate of about 8% per year between 1960 and 1980, thus altering the trend established from 1867 to 1948, when the money supply regularly grew more rapidly than nominal GNP.

There are real problems in defining the money supply, since the substitution possibilities among various types of financial assets are substantial. That is why various total money supplies are regularly presented and why the time series, even of a single aggregate, are revised from time to time—not unlike the problem of index numbers.

As recently as February 1980, the Fed "has redefined the monetary aggregates,"[4] largely because recent financial developments have further blurred the distinctions between thrift institutions and commercial banks. New monetary assets, such as NOW accounts, automatic transfer from savings accounts, credit union share draft balances, money market funds, and others have characteristics similar to checking accounts. Other assets, such as six- or twelve-month (or longer) denominated certificates of deposit (CDs), differ only marginally in terms of their degrees of "moneyness." In other words, "no one set of monetary aggregates can satisfy every purpose or every user."[5]

In short, there is no such thing as *the* money supply of the United States or any other country. The definition of money supply all depends on what one chooses to include in the definition of money. Since various financial assets have different degrees of "moneyness" (i.e., ease and cost of convertability into coin and currency), there can readily be many definitions of the money supply. In the United States in December 1979, for example, coin and currency held by the public totalled $106.3 billion; demand deposits at commercial banks, $263.4 billion (the sum of these two is now designated M_{1-A}); other checkable deposits at banks and thrift institutions, $16.7 billion (this plus M_{1-A} is now M_{1-B}); overnight repurchase agreements, $21.7 billion; overnight Eurodollars, $3.6 billion; money market mutual fund shares, $43.6 billion; savings and small (less than $100,000) time deposits at commercial banks and thrift institutions, $1,073.2 billion (these plus M_{1-B} now equal M_2); large (over $100,000)

TABLE 5.1

U.S. Money Supply[1] and Velocity[2] since 1960

Overall Measures ($billion)

	M_1	% Change	M_2	% Change	M_3	% Change	V_1	V_2	V_3
1960 Dec.	144.2		217.1		319.3		3.5	2.3	1.6
1961 "	148.7	3.1	228.6	5.3	342.1	7.1	3.5	2.3	1.5
1962 "	150.9	1.5	242.9	6.3	369.2	7.9	3.7	2.3	1.5
1963 "	156.5	3.7	258.9	6.6	400.3	8.4	3.8	2.3	1.5
1964 "	163.7	4.6	277.1	7.0	434.4	8.5	3.9	2.3	1.5
1965 "	171.4	4.7	301.4	8.8	471.8	8.6	4.0	2.3	1.5
1966 "	175.8	2.6	318.2	5.6	495.5	5.0	4.3	2.4	1.5
1967 "	187.4	6.6	350.0	10.0	544.0	9.8	4.3	2.3	1.5
1968 "	202.5	8.1	383.3	9.5	589.9	8.4	4.3	2.4	1.5
1969 "	209.0	3.2	392.4	2.4	607.4	3.0	4.5	2.3	1.5
1970 "	219.7	5.1	423.6	8.0	656.3	8.1	4.5	2.3	1.5
1971 "	233.9	6.5	471.8	11.4	745.1	13.5	4.6	2.3	1.4
1972 "	255.3	9.2	525.3	11.3	844.5	13.3	4.6	2.2	1.4
1973 "	270.5	6.0	571.3	8.8	919.0	8.8	4.8	2.3	1.4
1974 "	283.2	4.7	612.2	7.2	981.0	6.7	5.0	2.3	1.4
1975 "	295.4	4.3	664.8	8.6	1092.4	11.4	5.2	2.3	1.4
1976 "	313.8	6.2	740.6	11.4	1235.6	13.1	5.4	2.3	1.4
1977 "	338.7	7.9	809.4	9.3	1374.3	11.2	5.6	2.4	1.4
1978 "	361.5	6.7	879.0	8.6	1503.3	9.4	5.9	2.4	1.4
1979 "	382.1	5.7	952.6	8.4	1623.5	8.0	6.2	2.5	1.5

1. M_1 is currency plus demand deposits; M_2 is M_1 plus time and savings deposits at commercial banks other than large (over $100,000) CDs, plus checkable deposits at nonbank thrift institutions; M_3 is M_2 plus deposits at non-bank thrift institutions.

2. V_1 is nominal GNP ÷ M_1; V_2 is nominal GNP ÷ M_2; V_3 is nominal GNP ÷ M_3.

Source: Annual Report of the Council of Economic Advisers, U.S. Government Printing Office, Washington, D.C., 1980, table B-58 for money supply estimates and table B-1 for nominal GNP estimates.

time deposits, \$219.4 billion; term repurchase agreements, \$30.5 billion (these plus M_2 now equal M_3); and, finally, we have L, which is M_3 plus "other" liquid assets (savings bonds, short term treasury bills, bankers' acceptances, commercial paper, and term Eurodollars). For December 1979, the various definitions of the money supply, after several minor adjustments, were as follows:[6]

	\$billion
Coin and Currency	106.3
$M_{1\text{-A}}$	369.7
$M_{1\text{-B}}$	386.4
M_2	1,525.5
M_3	1,775.5
L	2,141.1

This enumeration is not intended to confuse but, rather, to highlight the point that there are many degrees of moneyness and, hence, many different but equally plausible definitions of the money supply. Prior to the creation of the Fed, for example, little distinction was possible between time and demand deposits. That distinction came with the creation of the Federal Reserve System and its differential reserve requirements between savings (time) and checking (demand) deposits. Thus, for earlier estimates of the money supply, the M_2 measure is necessary. With more recent developments and the possibility of shifting more easily from one type of financial asset to another (e.g., savings deposits in thrift institutions to CDs, savings deposits to checking deposits, and so on), the previous distinctions become blurred and, to some extent, meaningless. Therefore, a relatively slow growth in, say, $M_{1\text{-A}}$ may represent a shift out of checking accounts into savings accounts because of differential interest yields and may not have much economic significance at all. It may merely represent changes in the rules of the financial game that have been occurring with increasing frequency throughout the 1970s and culminating in the Depository Institutions Deregulation and Monetary Control Act of 1980. Relating a narrow definition of the money supply to another economic variable may yield a singularly distorted picture. "Money is as money does," goes the saying.

The several alternative definitions of the money supply, of course, also complicate the problems of the Fed in controlling the money supply, since the Federal Reserve System only has jurisdiction over commercial banks. Savings and loan associations are subject to the jurisdiction of the

Federal Home Loan Bank Board although since 1 January 1981, this has changed.

However, for the sake of carrying forward the discussion of the role of money, let us assume that there is one definition of the money supply, M (essentially M_{1-A}), and that the central bank has the duty to determine the level and especially the rate of change of M. How can this be done?

CONTROL OF THE MONEY SUPPLY

Most modern monetary systems operate on the basis of fractional reserves. That is, each commercial bank is required to keep on deposit with the Fed, or Central Bank in other countries, a specified fraction of its demand (and savings) deposit liabilities. Such a reserve ratio is normally in the 10–20% range, which can be altered from time to time, within specified limits, by the Fed. The total amount of money (coin and currency plus demand deposits, if we refer to M_1) thus depends on two things: the quantity of reserves (R) and the reserve ratio (r). Thus the potential money supply permitted by such a system is $M_p = \frac{R}{r}$. There are various complications and details with which we need not concern ourselves here since we are merely trying to outline the money control mechanism for those unfamiliar with its workings.[7]

Thus anything that changes R or r will alter the money supply. Initially, only the potential money supply will be affected, but since banks do not like to hold excess reserves, which pay no interest, sooner or later actual M will reach M_p. For example, if R = $1,000,000 and r = 10%, M_p = $10,000,000. If the Fed raises the reserve ratio to 15%, M_p would decline to $6,666,667 and, conversely, if r were reduced to say 8%, M_p would rise to $1,250,000. Frequent changes in the reserve ratio (r) tend, however, to be rather unsettling. The Fed thus has a more subtle way to influence M, namely by buying or selling mainly U.S. Government securities.

Let us assume that the Fed seeks to expand M. It can buy U.S. securities. It pays for these by writing a check against itself. The seller of these securities then deposits the check, say in the amount of $1,000, in some commercial bank. The bank gives the seller a demand deposit equal to $1,000 and sends the check to the Fed, which credits the bank with an increase in reserves (ΔR). The money supply has thus risen by $1,000. However, assuming the bank in question had no excess or de-

ficiency of reserves (i.e., its previous $\frac{R}{r}$ ratio equalled the legal requirements, say 10%), it now has excess reserves. Against the extra $1,000 in
deposits, it need only have extra reserves of $100—it has excess lending
power of $900. Since a bank lives by lending and is a profit-oriented
entity, it will be anxious to make loans totalling $900 on which it will
receive interest.

It will do this initially by increasing the deposits of the borrowers of
this $900, at the same time increasing its loan portfolio by the same
amount so that its balance sheet still balances. The business firms or
households borrowing this amount, of course, want to spend it on
something or they would not have borrowed it in the first place. They
then write a check or checks against the $900 deposit and give this to
the seller of the goods or services they wish to buy. The seller then deposits this in his bank, probably not the initial bank. This bank then
loses $900 of reserves and $900 of deposit liabilities as this check is pro-
cessed through the second bank.

The initial bank is now back in equilibrium—its reserves have increased by $100 (i.e., the initial $1,000 increase in reserves due to the
deposit by the seller of securities, less $900 deducted when the borrower's
check passes through the second bank), which is exactly 10% of the
$1,000 increase in deposit liabilities, and it has new loan assets of $900.
Its assets and liabilities have each risen by $1,000.

The second bank now has excess reserves (i.e., its $900 increase in
reserves against an increase in deposits of $900). It can lend out $810 in
a similar process as the first bank. Note that M has *now* increased by
$1,900 (the $1,000 increase in deposits at the first bank plus the $900
increase in deposits at the second bank).

The process will continue until the money supply has increased over
all by $10,000 in response to the increase in reserves of $1,000. Thus if
the initial situation were as above (total R = $1,000,000, r = 10%, and
M = $10,000,000), the injection into the system of an extra $1,000 in R
will lead to M = $\frac{1,001,000}{.10}$ = $10,010,000—an increase of $10,000. Total
new deposits created equal $\frac{\Delta R}{r}$.

The whole process goes into reverse when the Fed *sells* securities from
its portfolio. If the Fed wished to reduce M, it could sell $1,000 of securi-
ties, which would lead to a reduction in M of $10,000, assuming that
r equals 10%.

The Fed can therefore control the level and the rate of growth of the
money supply within reasonably narrow limits over any reasonable

length of time by so-called open market purchases and sales and by alter-ing the reserve ratio. Member banks of the Fed can also borrow reserves. The Fed can control or limit this by varying the interest rate it charges on such borrowed sums (called the discount rate) and by "moral sua-sion." But the primary technique is its use of open market operations.

Such deliberate changing of M, designed to offset inflation or unem-ployment, is called "monetary policy" (as noted in chapter 4) and is one of the major tools, along with fiscal policy, for attempting to facilitate economic stability and offset undesirable overall economic trends.

If the Fed is to play a constructive role in such endeavors, it must know how changes in the money supply affect real output (real GNP) and prices. We must therefore examine more closely the role of money. The following section examines the two major contending views concern-ing the importance of money in this process—the so-called Keynesian or fiscalist view, which stresses fiscal policy activism and the monetarist view, which stresses the role of money with special reference to inflation.

THE KEYNESIAN VIEW

In this view, the role of money, however defined, is indirect. The gen-eral view is that at any moment the public wants to hold a particular amount of their assets in the form of M. This demand to hold cash bal-ances depends on the rate of interest and the level of money income (nominal GNP). In general, the higher the rate of interest, the less money people choose to hold—and the smaller the proportion of peoples' assets will be held in the form of non-interest-earning assets such as money. At the same time, the higher the level of nominal income, the greater the amount of money needed for everyday transactions. Thus, the demand for M varies inversely with the interest rate and directly or posi-tively with the level of nominal income.

Any change in the supply of M, which can be deliberately engineered by the Fed, will thus set up a series of reactions. An increase in the money supply, which must be held by someone, say by an open market purchase, will—other things being equal—leave the public at large with more of their wealth in the form of a nonearning asset than they want. This will induce an attempt to exchange money for other interest-bear-ing assets (such as CDs or bonds). The increased purchase of such assets raises their price and reduces the rate of interest until the public as a whole chooses to hold the increased money supply at lower interest rates.

But the lower interest rates induce more investment spending and stimulate some more consumption spending as well, both of which raise nominal income (GNP at current prices). This in turn increases the demand for money. A new equilibrium will therefore be reached at higher levels of GNP, lower levels of interest, and a larger M. The opposite effects result from a decrease in M.

The impact of a change in the money supply on total spending is therefore indirect through its impact on the rate of interest. However, since a large number of studies in the late 1940s and 1950s indicated that neither investment nor consumption expenditures were particularly sensitive to interest rate changes, the view came to be held that monetary policy, which only controls the money supply directly and the interest rate indirectly, was not very effective. The most powerful and direct way to influence total spending was thus believed to be through changes in the tax rates (which directly altered disposable income and expected after-tax profitability for new investments) and/or public expenditures (which even more directly added to total spending). Fiscal policy became the preferred way to influence total expenditures and thus stabilize output and employment. Monetary policy was thereupon relegated to a subsidiary role, and more economists in the United States emphasized fiscal policy—hence the appellation "fiscalists."

THE MONETARIST VIEW

Those who emphasize the importance of money as a determinant of total spending, and thus of nominal GNP, start from what for several centuries has been known as the "equation of exchange." In the seventeenth century in England, for example, the notion that "plenty of money doth quicken trade" was pervasive. Indeed, the policy of what was then known as mercantilism was directed to obtaining a favorable balance of trade so that the export surplus would be paid in the form of gold and silver, thereby increasing the domestic money supply. "To sell more to strangers yearly than we consume of theirs in value"[8] became the criterion of whatever economic policy existed with its aim of increasing the money supply, since so-called modern methods of expanding M (as noted above) did not then exist.

But it was also believed that the general level of prices varied directly with the quantity of money. Thus inflation was directly linked to changes in M. The obvious inconsistency between this and the view that more money was desirable through a favorable balance of trade was by and large lost on the mercantilists. Indeed, it was not until David Hume (1752), the great English philosopher, unraveled the inconsistency that clearer views of the importance of money became established.[9]

By the end of the nineteenth century, long after the mercantilists' policies had been demolished by Adam Smith and the role of the money supply relegated to one of utter insignificance by the so-called classical economists, a more complete version of the theory of exchange was elucidated. This broke total spending up into two components, the money supply (M) and its average velocity of circulation (V). Since total purchases (MV) must necessarily equal total sales, with the latter decomposed into P (the price level) multiplied by the physical level of output (O), or real GNP, it then follows that:

$$MV = PO.$$

This is true by definition, of course, and thus explains nothing any more than the truism that GNP $= C + I + G + NFI$. Furthermore, by limiting O to real GNP, we define V as PO divided by M, or $V = \frac{PO}{M}$, from which it also follows that $MV = PO$. If, then, V is relatively constant, nominal income (PO or nominal GNP) varies directly with changes in M.

It would appear, then, assuming V or the demand for money to be relatively stable, that slowing the rate of growth of M, as the Fed is currently attempting, can be an effective way of curbing inflation, especially in an economy close to the full employment level. Of course, raising taxes and decreasing total spending can have the same effect. We have, however, noted the serious difficulties in implementing short-run fiscal policies and especially the unwillingness of politicians to raise taxes rather than lower them. Thus policies of fiscal activism may be singularly inappropriate to offset short-run cyclical instability, particularly when it comes to inflationary pressures. All too often during the late 1960s and the 1970s, fiscal policy affected the economy well after the recovery had begun and thus contributed more to inflationary pressures than to further real output increases. The problem of time lags and the relative shortness of recessions over the past two decades may have made any policy of "fine tuning" the economy virtually impossible.[10].

Monetarists and others therefore stress the importance of the money supply and hence monetary policy as a stabilizing device rather than fiscal policy. But monetary policy is subject to similar types of lags as fiscal policy although the implementation lag is generally shorter. In addition, if the inflation fight is mainly left to a tight monetary policy, interest rates will rise sharply and the availability of credit, especially to consumers, will be severely restricted. Thus the automobile industry and especially the housing industry will be seriously affected, an unintended side effect of such a policy.

In terms of many lags, uncertainties, and side effects, neither policy has any clear-cut net intrinsic superiority over the other in principle.

As the Report of the Joint Economic Committee put it, with special reference to the 1980 recession and recovery:

> The delays in implementing a government action in the case of fiscal policy and the lags in transmitting actions to employment and production in the cases of (both) fiscal and monetary policy suggest that most of the effects of actions taken during a recession will occur during the recovery rather than during the recession. Therefore, attempts to shorten the present recession through fiscal or monetary initiatives should take these lags into account. The delay in recognizing a downturn means that the recession is partly over before a decision can be made to respond to it. . . . The uncertainties surrounding the issue of how government actions influence the business cycle are, if anything, more pronounced with respect to monetary policy. There is no consensus among economists and other experts as to how monetary policy affects the economy.[11]

OTHER DIFFERENCES

Not only the relative importance of the change in M separates the Keynesians from the monetarists. Indeed, on a more fundamental level, there are differences about the *sources* of instability of a market-oriented economy and the *extent* of any inherent instability. Monetarists view the economy as substantially more stable than do Keynesians. Indeed, it is no accident that much of Keynesian economics emerged as a result of trying to explain the Great Depression. The collapse of private investment between 1929 and 1933 when it declined by 88% (see table 4.1) was viewed as further evidence of the instability of this component of GNP and thus a leading cause of the severity of the decline. The volatility of consumer durable expenditures, because of their postponable nature, also contributes to overall instability of the private sector. Compensatory public spending and/or tax changes were thus believed necessary to offset such instability.

However, the monetarist explanation of the severity of the Great Depression lies in the sharp contraction of the money supply by some 30% between 1929 and 1933 and the belief that this "was a direct consequence of the policies followed by the Federal Reserve System."[12] The stress here is not on the severe reduction in the *demand* for loans (as a result of any collapse of business confidence, which Keynesians tend to stress), but to the shrinking of the money supply. Thus, it was the Fed's actions (or inactions), along with a perverse fiscal policy (see chapter 4, Introduction), that made the Great Depression so severe. Without these actions, the economy, it is alleged, would have exhibited no more than the kind of instability experienced earlier (and presumably subsequently).

In terms of the *ability* of either the Fed or fiscal policy authorities to implement sensible policies, there is widespread disagreement. Keynesians, though somewhat disillusioned with the policy actions during the 1960s and 1970s, still believe that deliberate, ad hoc actions are needed due to various demand and supply-side shocks and the asymmetry of the business cycle. They therefore support a higher degree of discretionary monetary and fiscal policy than do the monetarists. Mistakes will be and have been made, as noted earlier, but, on balance, it is believed that such activist and discretionary policies have contributed to the far higher degree of stability of Western economies in the post–World War II era than earlier. They point to the Hungry Forties (1840s) so vividly portrayed by Charles Dickens in his novels, the long worldwide recession from 1873 to the 1890s, and other "hard times" as evidence that passivity of public economic policy merely accentuates instability, when the aim should be to offset it (as previously argued in chapter 4) in the context of an annually balanced federal budget.

Monetarists tend to believe that the difficulties associated with implementing sensible and effective monetary and fiscal policies are so great, for reasons previously noted, that they should not even be attempted. They often stress the need for "rules" rather than discretion. They believe, for example, that the Fed should be required to change the money supply at a more or less constant rate per year (say 4%) and that attempts to "fine tune" the economy on a short-run basis by sudden shifts in the rate of growth of M cause more instability and uncertainty than would be the case with a steadier course.

The monetarist emphasis is on both our inadequate knowledge of how the economy functions and the unwillingness or inability of the Fed, and especially Congress, to act sensibly and with dispatch, even if the economy were sounder. Fiscal policy in particular, with its long implementation lag, has often led to tax changes that were too little, too late or too much, too soon. Our forecasting ability in an uncertain world is simply not capable of providing a solid basis for an activist fiscalism. Even monetary policy suffers from a relatively long and variable impact lag in prices (Friedman estimates 12–18 months; others estimate two years, or more). This very uncertainty and variability suggest the need for a steadier course.

It is these different perceptions of reality, rather than basic analytical differences, that underlie the differing policy recommendations of these two broad approaches. In this sense it is less a matter of right or wrong but, rather, one of relative emphasis: emphasis on monetary versus fiscal policy; emphasis on rules versus discretion.

But, finally, there are differences concerning the importance of the short run versus the long run. Keynesians tend to favor the short run (as Keynes once said, "In the long run we are all dead")—unemployment and/or inflation should therefore be addressed promptly. Monetarists tend to favor the long run and believe that short-run attempts to reduce unemployment will simply lead to more unemployment later.

Yet nobody knows how long the long run is. Friedman has suggested that "in the short run, which may be as much as five or ten years, monetary changes affect primarily output" and hence unemployment.[13] On the other hand, "over decades, the rate of monetary growth affects primarily prices."[14] Others make different estimates of the relative length of the short run and the long run.

In an economy subject to elections at two-year and four-year intervals, this ambiguity about policies—how long it would take and with which policies to reduce inflation and at what cost in terms of unemployment or reduced output—creates serious problems for policy.

There are then several issues of contention regarding the fiscalists and monetarists. These are (1) the relative importance of the money supply, (2) the degree of inherent instability of the economy in the absence of activist policy, and (3) the issue of rules versus discretion.

WHAT THE EVIDENCE AND ANALYSIS SHOW

The Relative Importance of Money

In chapter 2 I noted that much of the evidence, spotty as it is, indicated that changes in the money supply (associated with debasement of the currency, a sharp influx of gold and silver, and so on) were historically associated with rising prices. At the same time, the hyperinflations reviewed in that chapter indicated the importance of changes in the rate of spending (V) of the money supply. The monetarist position is largely based on the stability of the "demand for money" function in the sense that society as a whole chooses, for various levels of income, to retain a certain proportion of its assets in the form of real balances ($\frac{M}{P}$). Thus, as indicated in the Keynesian formulation, a change in M by deliberate policy changes actual $\frac{M}{P}$ from the desired level. This change induces a set of reactions that influence both prices (P) and real output (O).

For example, if M increases, people find themselves holding more real balances than desired. They then buy more goods, services, stocks, bonds, CDs, and so on. This will raise the price of whatever is purchased in the immediate run. If the economy has enough excess capacity, the increased spending will raise output after a brief lag. On the other hand, if there is little excess capacity, the impact of the increased spending associated with a rise in M will be largely in the form of price increases. The division between real output increases and price increases is then the important consideration as far as inflation is concerned.

How much of the increased spending induced by an increase in M is devoted to real output (and employment) increases and how much to price increases? The rate of growth of total spending is the sum of the rate of growth of prices and of output. Thus, if prices rise by 10% and real output rises by 2%, the total increase in spending is 12%. I have already noted (chapter 4) that increased spending during the Great Depression resulted in a far greater proportion of output increase than price increase whereas the opposite typified the situation of the 1970s. The difference, of course, was the degree of excess capacity in the economy between the two dates.

Thus, one of the keys to the role of an increase in the rate of growth of M on inflation is its impact on spending and the degree of excess capacity or the level of unemployment. If there is plenty of excess capacity or high unemployment, the output effect will dominate the price effect and vice versa (see figure 2.1).

The problem, then, is to determine how an increase in M affects total spending and then to decide how this is distributed between output increases and price increases. If V, the velocity of circulation, is stable, then in the equation of exchange nominal income (total spending) will increase directly and proportionately with changes in M. Evidence of this since 1960 is shown in table 5.2.

TABLE 5.2

Nominal Income and Changes in M_1 and M_2

Year	Nominal GNP $billions	% Change	M_1 as of Dec. $billions	% Change	M_2 as of Dec. $billions	% Change
1960	506.0		144.2		217.1	
1961	523.3	3.4	148.7	3.1	228.6	5.3
1962	563.8	7.7	150.9	1.5	242.9	6.3
1963	594.7	5.5	156.5	3.7	258.9	6.6
1964	635.7	6.9	163.7	4.6	277.1	7.0
1965	688.1	8.2	171.4	4.7	301.4	8.8
1966	753.0	9.4	175.8	2.6	318.2	5.6
1967	796.3	5.8	187.4	6.6	350.0	10.0
1968	868.5	9.1	202.5	8.1	383.3	9.5
1969	935.5	7.7	209.0	3.2	392.4	2.4
1970	982.4	5.0	219.7	5.1	423.6	8.0
1971	1,063.4	8.2	233.9	6.5	471.8	11.4
1972	1,171.1	10.1	255.3	9.1	525.3	11.3
1973	1,306.6	11.6	270.5	6.0	571.3	8.8
1974	1,412.9	8.1	283.2	4.7	612.2	7.2
1975	1,528.8	8.2	295.4	4.4	664.8	8.6
1976	1,702.2	11.3	313.8	6.2	740.6	11.4
1977	1,899.5	11.6	338.7	7.9	809.4	9.3
1978	2,127.6	12.0	361.5	6.7	879.0	8.6
1979	2,368.5	11.3	382.1	5.7	952.6	8.4

There is a very high correlation between nominal GNP and either M_1 or M_2. This is partially spurious since both series have been increasing steadily over time and the direction of causation is not unambiguous. Does a high and rising nominal GNP cause or induce the Fed to raise the money supply, or does a high and rising money supply cause high and rising nominal GNP? Most economists, both Keynesian and monetarist, would argue the latter.

The data in table 5.2 indicate that there is no proportionality between changes on a year-to-year basis for nominal GNP and either M_1 or M_2. Sometimes the percentage change in nominal GNP exceeds that of M_1 or M_2 and sometimes the reverse is true. Nor should any strict proportionality be expected, since the impact of a change in M takes time to work itself out—the issue of the impact lag once again. Yet relating changes in nominal GNP to changes in M_1 or M_2 one year earlier reveals no consistent pattern. Although the variation of the ratio of the percentage change of GNP in one year to the percentage change of M_1 or M_2 in

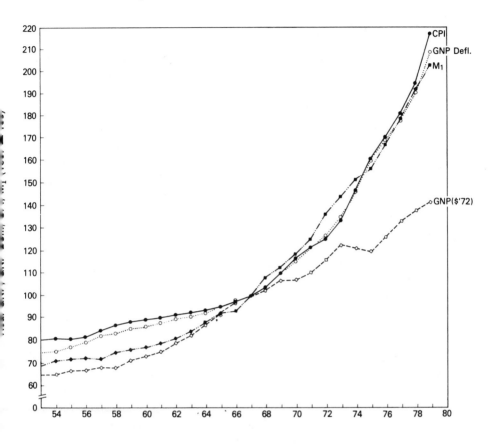

Fig. 5.2   Trends in the Money Supply, Consumer Price Index, and
Real and Nominal GNP, 1953–1979

the previous year is somewhat less volatile,[15] the range of variation is
substantial.

Some evidence concerning the relationship between money and prices
is presented in figure 5.2. When we graph the behavior of M (the M_1
version) alongside movements of the Consumer Price Index and the
GNP deflator, both widely used inflation indicators, the closeness of the
relationship is immediately apparent.[16]

The relationship of M_1 to real GNP also appears reasonably close up
to 1967 but thereafter diverges markedly, with M_1 rising far more rapid-

ly than real GNP. This indicates that the impact of money supply increases have shown up increasingly in the form of price increases rather
than output increases—which supports the earlier version of the crude
quantity of money theory, namely that prices vary directly with the supply of money as full capacity of the economy is approached.

Data on the velocity of circulation, shown in table 5.1, indicate a high
degree of stability, especially for V_2 and V_3. V_1 has exhibited a fairly
steady upward drift, especially since the early 1970s. This trend is largely
associated with the higher yields obtainable from nonchecking deposits
and the decreasing distinction between checking deposits and other forms
of deposit (CDs or money market funds yielding higher interest rates).

The implication of this table is that money *does* matter and that perhaps it matters in a fashion somewhat more directly than in the earlier
Keynesian view, which argued that a change in M changed interest rates
in the opposite direction and that interest rates influenced investment
spending and, to a lesser extent, consumption spending. As noted earlier,
the belief that neither investment nor consumption expenditures were
especially sensitive to interest rate changes led to a de-emphasis on M and
monetary policy. This was reinforced by the notion that in a recession,
business confidence, deemed the major determinant of investment, was
so low that the demand for loans would simply not be there regardless
of the degree of excess reserves in the banking system. Since the Fed's
main weapon of monetary expansion or contraction involved the creation or elimination of reserves, monetary policy was considered relatively
impotent to induce a recovery. On the other hand, the Fed could readily
choke off an expansion by tight money. As the Fed once put it, "It is
easier to pull on a string than push."

In addition, it is no longer clear that an increase in M will lower
interest rates. For example, if it is believed that an increase in M will
raise the rate of inflation, interest rates may well rise, not fall. Monetarists in particular stress the difference between nominal and real rates
of interest. The real rate of interest is the nominal rate less the rate of
inflation. Lenders are presumably interested in real rates of interest.
Why should one loan funds at, say, 5% if the rate of inflation is 5%?
There would be no gain whatsoever to compensate for the risk and
trouble of lending.

Thus, if a rise in M leads to expectations of an associated rise in the
inflation rate, nominal interest rates will probably rise, not fall. In an
era of high inflation, the distinction between nominal and real rates of
interest takes on new importance, as does the influence of expectations.

Borrowers are likewise interested in real interest rates. If one can borrow at 5% with actual or anticipated inflation rates of more than that, the temptation to borrow, spend, enjoy, and then repay in dollar amounts of significantly less real value is difficult to resist. Inflation stimulates shortsightedness, as we discuss more fully later.

In fact, recently the credit markets are reacting (in the short run to be sure) as if a sharp increase in the money supply beyond the Fed's targets were inflationary and thus would raise, not lower, short-term rates. "Good news" is when the rate of growth of the money supply is sharply down. This is a perverse case of the law of supply and demand due to expectations. An increase in supply (of money and credit) leads to an increase in price (the short-term interest rate) and vice versa. This does not usually happen in other markets.

The Instability of the Market System

The past experience with most market oriented economies indicates a relatively high degree of cyclical instability beginning in England following the end of the Napoleonic wars in 1815. Waves of expansion and contraction appeared to be inherent in the economy during the next hundred years. In some respects, this was the heyday of laissez-faire, when governments were relatively small and were expected to balance budgets regularly. Monetary "policy" in any activist sense was virtually nonexistent. The money supply was tied to gold and the best the central bank or banking system could do was to be neutral. That is, not to do anything foolish, such as overexpand the currency, because this did have adverse consequences—especially as far as the foreign trade balance was concerned. But, at best, money and banking could only facilitate trade; at worst, they could disrupt it.

So regular appeared to be the business cycle that some even attributed its cause to "sunspots," which themselves, at the time, appeared at regular intervals. After a while, the business cycle came to be taken as almost a law of nature. What goes up must come down. Karl Marx based much of his condemnation of the capitalistic system not only on the alleged exploitation of the working class but on the system's apparently inherent instability. Indeed, the Marxian prediction of the ultimate demise of the system itself lay in an analysis that indicated increasingly severe crises (recessions or depressions) that would sooner or later create a situation of such massive unemployment that the collective power of the unemployed would enable them to seize the instruments of production and later usher in the communist state. Capitalism was but a transitory phase in the economic and social evolution of societies.

Later, in the nineteenth and early twentieth centuries, business cycle "theories" began to emerge. Certain distortions or contradictions appeared in the expansion phase in market economies. New investments—induced in the early stages by low interest rates, new technologies, or some factor that improves profit prospects—generate incomes, raise consumption spending, and initially increase prices. Profit margins widen as the labor force gets absorbed in producing the increased output at stable wage rates because of the initially high unemployment rate. Interest rates lag because of large excess reserves in the banking system. But, as the expansion continues, the economy absorbs the excess labor and excess reserves. Further expansion generates high wages and interest rates. Other production costs may rise as selective "bottlenecks" occur.

At the same time, the earlier investments begin to pour forth more goods. Prices begin to soften as production costs rise. Profit margins get squeezed. "It's harder to make a buck" is a statement at this stage frequently heard in the business community. The squeeze on profits leads to some losses and bankruptcies. Some banks even fail, leaving their depositors with sharply reduced purchasing power. Consumption increases slow down. The expected markets don't materialize. Pessimism sets in among the business community. New investments are postponed or cancelled, no longer justified due to higher interest rates and/or dimmed sales and profit prospects.

A net contraction in economic activity occurs. Unemployment rises and wages and prices fall in a pure market system, as the economy unravels in a downward spiral. But this, too, is self-correcting, as wages and other production costs begin to fall faster than prices, thereby raising profit margins. Low interest rates may encourage new investment, which raises incomes and spending. And so the expansion begins all over again and the process repeats itself. All of this is obviously affected by major external events such as wars (a Marxist would argue that this is an internal event and one of the major ways capitalism recovers from the periodic crises of overproduction), crop failures, supply cutoffs, financial panics, etc. But, given freely flexible prices including wages, the system will always recover if left alone. It is, however, uniquely susceptible to waves of optimism and pessimism (especially of the business community), which are both cause and consequence of the foregoing cycles.

All during the nineteenth century and especially the twentieth after World War II, real economic growth was being achieved within the capitalistic system but not elsewhere at rates never before recorded in human history over such a sustained period. The business cycle was believed to be an inevitable—indeed necessary—accompaniment of rising standards of living. And living standards, on the average, did in fact increase greatly in the capitalist world. True, so did inequality of income distribution up to about 1850, but the gains from investments associated with independent entrepreneurs responding to market forces, accrued to the population at large, though by differential amounts. Instability and inequality were widely perceived as the price of progress.

After the Keynesian revolution, which saw itself as a non-Marxian alternative to achieve both continued economic growth and greater stability without throwing over the best features of capitalism, more sophisticated cyclical theories were developed. I shall not document these here, but the net implication was to reinforce the previously perceived inherent instability[17] in the absence of deliberate policies designed to offset it.

Empirical studies of the cycle were begun in earnest by Professor Wesley Clair Mitchell and the National Bureau of Economic Research in the early 1900s which also broadly confirmed a sort of "rhythm of business."

The Great Depression, however, came as a shock due to its severity and duration. Most Western democracies made conscious decisions not to let it happen again and deliberately created certain "built-in stabilizers." Such measures as unemployment compensation and progressive income taxes would automatically insure a government deficit during contraction and a surplus during expansion. These effects would tend to blunt both the depths of contraction and the heights of expansion (or inflation, if the expansion of spending began to exceed capacity). But since each cycle always had certain unique features associated with it, a somewhat more activist and ad hoc policy seemed to be called for.

Thus in the United States, the Employment Act of 1946 was passed, which pledged the federal government to maintain high levels of employment and stable prices. The methods were to be monetary and fiscal policies, indirect policies falling far short of the socialist cries for detailed overall planning and extensive public ownership.

In short, in the absence of countercyclical monetary and fiscal policies and built-in stabilizers, both the evidence of some 150 years as well as analysis suggest that the market system is inherently unstable. The extent of such instability has been pronounced unacceptable by democratic societies and the need for countercyclical policies widely accepted. To this extent, we are all Keynesians now.

The Issue of Rules vs. Discretion

Keynesians view the private sector as inherently unstable—probably seriously unstable, serious at least in the sense of being politically unacceptable. When unemployment rates rise much above 5 or 6%, "something" needs to be done. When the inflation rate approaches the double-digit level, again something needs to be done. When the two undesirable situations coincide, the "something" that needs to be done becomes very complex. More than mere aggregate demand management may be necessary.

Monetarists, on the other hand, argue that the private sector is much more stable than Keynesians presume and that the observed cyclical instability in the past has, in fact, been caused by the public sector. Changes in bank reserves have been observed to precede or coincide with major cyclical turning points. Fiscal policy and changes therein have often aggravated instability rather than offset it.

The Keynesian arguments imply an activist policy designed to "lean against the wind." The government is viewed as the "balance wheel" of an inherently unstable system. The monetarist view implies a steady—or at least steadier—monetary and fiscal policy: specifically, a balanced federal budget at "full employment" and a growth in the money supply consistent with the growth in the "capacity" of the economy to produce. Frequent changes in tax rates, government spending, and/or the money supply are themselves destabilizing. This is partly due to the problem of lags, our inability to forecast with much accuracy, and the ever-present problem of politics in formulating sensible stabilization policies.

The issue of rules versus discretion thus boils down to the past sources of instability in a market economy and the ability of government to respond to such cyclical movements, some of which government policy may have initiated or aggravated.

Yet devising a tax structure and level, combined with a federal spending program that would be in balance if the economy were at full employment, is a difficult undertaking even if we could define full employment unambiguously. In an economy subject to apparently ever-increasing external shocks, the need to respond to mitigate the effects of such shocks is apparent. Some degree of discretionary behavior appears necessary. Passivity in the face of this type of often unpredictable occurrences is hardly appealing and, indeed, is quite unrealistic to expect. Mistakes will be, and have been, made. Policymakers are fallible human beings. Whether the costs of such mistakes would exceed the costs of passivity in the face of either inherent instability or unanticipated events, cannot, of course, be calculated with any accuracy. However, we have learned from past mistakes and presumably will continue to learn more and more about the impacts of policy. It is doubtful whether a set of rules could be devised that would be appropriate under all circumstances.

However, a real dilemma of any activist monetary and fiscal policy is the persistence of high inflation rates in the face of high and variable unemployment rates. But any set of fixed rules faces a similar dilemma. If we succeed in bringing down both the rate of inflation and unemployment, with all of their measurement and interpretive problems, to more acceptable levels (say, 4% or 5% each), it is clear that the sensible course of action would be a steadier policy. Both Keynesians and monetarists could agree under these conditions. But, in addition, it is apparent that some of the policy changes of the late 1960s and 1970s represented more or less visceral reactions to very short-run disturbances—disturbances that very likely would have reversed themselves in short order. A longer range view of policy actions should prevail in the future, now that the belief in "fine tuning" has been shattered.

6 The Consequences of Inflation

INTRODUCTION

Inflation, as defined in chapter 1, is a persistent rise in some general index of prices that, due to expectations, becomes self-supporting. Yet not *all* prices rise, nor do they rise by the same extent. Inflation therefore results in a form of income and wealth redistribution totally unrelated to any desirable goal of either economic or social policy. Thus there are losers as well as winners, in a relative sense, whenever inflation persists. Let us now attempt to sort out the winners and the losers.

However, before turning to this issue, there are various aggregative or general implications of inflation that must be stressed. Even if all prices rose by the same or similar proportions, there would be several macroeconomic repercussions.

In the first place, if the inflation rate exceeded that of other nations, exports would tend to decrease and imports increase as the relative prices of domestic goods began to exceed those of foreign goods. This situation would worsen the balance of trade and put downward pressure on the value of the dollar. In the short run, unemployment would rise, which should reduce the rate of inflation. The decrease in the value of the dollar relative to other currencies should reduce the imbalance between exports and imports. In this sense, the balance of trade would be self-correcting over time. If nothing else intervened to sustain the inflation rate domestically and if domestic prices were free to fall, the international imbalance would correct itself. However, the latter two assumptions are unrealistic. The adjustment process is also subject to lags of uncertain duration. The impact of domestic inflation rates higher than those of America's major trading partners is thus likely to lead to considerable and prolonged problems with respect to the international sector, which is growing rapidly as a proportion of U.S. GNP.

If persistent inflation occurs, there will be distortions in resource allocation away from longer term productive investments and toward assets such as housing, inventories, real estate, gold, rare paintings, and the like. Such assets are unproductive in the sense that they don't yield higher real output per unit of input in the future. Savings will therefore tend to be allocated in ways that inhibit the future capacity to grow.

Inflation also promotes shortsightedness, because few inflation rates are steady from period to period. Thus, under inflationary conditions, predicting future costs and profits that might be reaped by a proposed new productive investment (say a steel mill or a power plant) becomes more risky than normal. Add to this the higher nominal interest rate that always accompanies inflation, and we not only have a set of conditions promoting shortsightedness, but also a positive discouragement to any new productive investment at all. Certainly, a large part of the explanation of sluggish real investment in business plant and equipment over the past decade in the United States and elsewhere is due to the impact of inflation.

In a very real sense, these macro impacts of inflation tend to reinforce the inflation process. The "great productivity slowdown" in the United States means that unit production costs are higher than otherwise, and these will quickly be transmitted to the price level. In short, the productivity offset to rising money wages, material, and resource costs dwindles as a result of inflation itself.[1]

Another distortion that has been widely cited in the United States is "income tax bracket creep." As personal incomes rise, even if only enough to keep up with the rising prices, the progressive income tax system ensures that the effective tax rate will rise. This rise tends to discourage productive effort. Indeed, to offset bracket creep, individuals will devote an inordinate amount of time and resources to purely financial dealings, seeking new exemptions, and so on, thus reducing overall productivity still further. In addition, with high rates of inflation, we get high nominal rates of interest. Thus the cost of holding one's assets in the form of non-interest-bearing money induces people to put most of their money in the form of some type of interest-earning asset. This, in turn, requires frequent funds transfers to meet current obligations and/ or more frequent trips to the bank for cash. Some have referred to this as "shoe leather costs" of high inflation.

A similar bracket creep problem occurs with respect to business profits. Those firms basing depreciation estimates on historical or original costs and/or who use the first-in, first-out method of accounting for the value of inventory change, will experience illusory profits and pay higher taxes

on them. Such firms will not accumulate enough funds over time to replace their existing capital stocks, let alone expand or replace them with
superior (i.e., more productive) capital equipment. This problem also
jeopardizes new investment.

In countries where the government owns or controls many public utilities in which prices tend to be fixed—or at least not allowed to change
with the inflation rate (e.g., fares on urban transit systems, railroad
freight rates, and other public utilities)—a self-reinforcing inflationary
tendency occurs. The deficits arising in such enterprises need to be made
up by the central government, thereby increasing its deficit. To finance
this deficit, the money supply is normally increased—an action which
itself reinforces inflation, which further accentuates deficits, and so on
it goes.

A similar self-perpetuating phenomenon obtains in those countries that
hold down or actually subsidize the price of a major import (oil in the
United States, for example). Holding down the price encourages use.
This aggravates the balance of payments situation, which often leads to
devaluation. The devaluation leads to higher import prices all around
and, unless imports are sharply curtailed, will contribute to domestic
inflation.

In short, even if most prices went up at similar rates, there would be
serious difficulties, especially in the context of further real growth, or
high and persistent inflation. Such difficulties often lead governments to
control one or more prices, which in turn tends to reinforce inflationary
pressures. There is merit and necessity in trying to bring down the rate
of inflation even though, under some circumstances (such as those in
Brazil, noted in chapter 2) "growth by inflation" may be experienced for
a limited period. Certainly, these special circumstances did not and will
not prevail in the United States of the 1970s and 1980s.

There is one more problem even with an inflation in which all prices
rise by the same amount. That is, Can any high rate of inflation be contained at its current level? The status of expectations may change, and
a more or less steady rate of inflation may accelerate, ultimately leading
to the kind of hyperinflation (with all its consequences) experienced by
Germany after World War I. However, the usual emphasis on the "evils
of inflation" refers to the relative income and wealth transfers that accompany all inflations, since all prices do not rise by the same or even
similar amounts.

WINNERS AND LOSERS FROM HIGH INFLATION RATES

Income Redistribution

Obviously, all those whose incomes rise faster than the average gain relative to those whose incomes lag behind the overall inflation rate. The former gain in real purchasing power, while the latter rose. As Keynes long ago remarked, one of the major consequences of inflation is the "euthanasia of the rentier"—the mercy killing of all those living on a fixed income. The crucial question is, who are the winners (the nonrentiers) and losers (the quasi rentiers) as far as real incomes are concerned? People or households whose income is fixed in monetary terms or whose incomes depend on contracts spanning several years and not subject to either indexing or renegotiation will clearly suffer most. This would include many pensioners (but not social security recipients, since social security benefits are indexed) and those whose bargaining power is weak, such as the poor and unskilled, casual workers.

Nevertheless, it is not easy to identify the winners and losers in terms of rich versus poor. One study did find that in the overall income distribution, both the lower and upper ends lost relative shares to the middle range of the income distribution for unanticipated increases in the inflation rate.[2] The magnitude of the redistribution was, however, small. On a more aggregative basis, involving the changing shares of national income going to the various income categories (wages, profits, rents, etc.), somewhat more dramatic shifts have been reported.[3] Contrary to conventional expectations, the wages and salaries share of national income appears to rise during inflationary periods at the same time corporate profits' share decreases. Transfer payments also tend to rise as a proportion of national income, suggesting that the poor and the elderly may not suffer relatively in a period of inflation. Yet these findings did not include the inflationary period from 1976 through 1979, when the rate of increase of both the CPI and GNP deflator rose steadily on a year-to-year basis. The changes in the income shares noted for earlier inflations were mostly reversed. Specifically, wages and salaries *decreased* as a proportion of national income, as did transfer payments; corporate profits also declined. The other income categories (interest, rents, and proprietors' income) all rose slightly, contrary to the experience since 1965 during U.S. inflationary periods.[4]

It is not, therefore, clear that serious income redistributions away from the poor to the rich do in fact accompany high rates of inflation. Yet, during episodes of stagflation, small businesses fare much worse than larger enterprises. Even in a strictly inflationary situation, small firms, always more reliant on credit at higher nominal interest rates than large firms and usually with narrower profit margins, are especially disadvantaged. This tendency has obvious antitrust implications and is one of many reasons for not relying strictly on monetary policy to contain inflation.

However, in terms of personal income and its distribution, the impact of inflation is much more ambiguous. One clear winner in the inflation process is the federal government, along with all those state governments having a progressive income tax or a fixed property tax with frequent value reassessments. Revenues burgeon because of "bracket creep" or higher property reassessments. The incentive for governments to raise spending appears to be virtually irresistible, and, obviously, tax rate reductions would further aggravate inflation. In fact, most of the tax rate reductions during the 1970s led to increased government revenues—not so much because they spurred economic activity but more because they aggravated inflation and inflation expectations. From 1971 to the present, federal revenues from the personal income tax have risen every year despite the slump in 1974–75 and the tax reductions then and later as outlined in chapter 4. Yet the annual average real growth rate was only 3.3%, compared with an inflation rate averaging 6.8% (implicit GNP deflator) or 7.6% (CPI).

In general, the evidence concerning personal income distribution in the postwar United States indicates "that the overall position of the poor, relative to the positions of other groups, is likely to improve during phases of inflation—so long as these phases are combined with tight labor markets and not of the 'stagflation type.' "[5] The latter caveat and some offsetting private and public policies are what makes it so difficult to ascertain the effects on the income distribution. Incomes of the poor or middle class fall when unemployment rises. With rising prices, especially of basic necessities, their purchasing power falls even more. But this is at least partially compensated by private and public offsetting unemployment or supplemental unemployment benefits. The net impact on the *real* incomes of the poor relative to that of the middle or upper income groups is difficult to disentangle in terms of broad categories of income recipients. As recently concluded, "labor's share (of national income) is largely unaffected by inflation on the average, though individual wages may outpace or fall behind prices."[6] For the rich, a greater part of whose income comes from interest or dividend payments, real incomes are liable to fall somewhat unless nominal interest rates rise faster than the price level. Dividends tend to lag. Yet for lower or middle income groups, whose interest and dividend income is probably modest in the first place, the need to rely on passbook savings rates (hitherto fixed by Reg. Q of the Federal Reserve System), real interest, and possibly dividends, becomes negative. Passbook savings at $5\frac{1}{2}\%$ with inflation at 10–14% is no bargain—in fact it represents a $4\frac{1}{2}$ to $8\frac{1}{2}\%$ loss. Nor are many of the poor or even middle class able to take advantage of the large money market CDs or other instruments. Recently, this has begun to change. But in the past, the lower to middle income groups saw their savings dissipated by inflation rates in the 5 to 15% range.

However, in terms of income distribution, the impact of the higher than usual rates of inflation we have experienced in the late 1960s and all of the 1970s, depends on the particular mix of income sources, the extent to which each is indexed or supplemented, in the case of stagflation, by unemployment benefits. Particular families or households may be seriously affected, while for others the impact is negligible, and for some, beneficial. Again, the impact will reflect the different rates of inflation of the various components of, say, the CPI. If inflation rates are highest in what may be deemed "necessities" (food, shelter, medical care), other things being equal, the lower one's income, the greater the proportion of one's budget spent on necessities: hence the greater the negative impact of inflation.

In general, inflation is a form of taxation. Its incidence, however, depends on a large number of characteristics not only of the inflation itself but of the income sources and expenditure patterns of households. It is thus difficult to come up with any generalization as to the overall quantitative impact of inflation on the redistribution of income; it is more difficult still to spell out which specific groups of income recipients are relative winners or losers.

In the long run, I have no doubt that we all lose due to the adverse macroeconomic impacts discussed above. And there is no gainsaying the fact that whatever income redistributions occur are random and not related to any explicit or implicit social, economic, or even political purpose. Whether inflation is the "cruelest tax of all," as has been said, is certainly debatable unless one refers to galloping inflations such as those which occurred in Brazil and Germany. The U.S. inflation of the past 15 years is far from galloping—it varies sharply from year to year with little evidence of secular trend. While this fluctuation causes more diffi-

culties and distortions than a steady-state inflation, and while a steady
state and lower rate of inflation would be preferable, the current situation is far from disastrous. It could, however, become so if steps are not
taken to accomplish both steadier overall rates of price change and to
lower the rate at least to the 4 or 5% range.

Wealth Redistribution

The most obvious redistribution of wealth (i.e., shifts in the value of
financial assets vis-à-vis liabilities), as distinguished from income, is that
between creditors and debtors. Creditors are those who hold cash, bank
accounts, savings deposits (all liabilities of the Fed, banks, or savings
institutions), or bonds (usually liabilities of governments and businesses).
Bank accounts (at least until 1 January 1981) received no interest, nor
did cash. Thus when the price level rises, their *real* purchasing power
declines. Savings and bonds, in whatever form, do receive interest, but if,
as is usually the case, the rate of interest is below the rate of inflation,
real incomes decrease. On the asset side, the real value of any given
amount of savings or bonds that are redeemable in specified money
amounts, clearly decreases with inflation.

Thus, creditors or those who lend or hold money, suffer a wealth loss
due to inflation. The purchasing power of their assets when due or
cashed is less than when they were made or acquired, unless they have
been indexed or otherwise adjusted via higher yields to account for anticipated inflation. On the other side of the coin, the borrowers gain
since they repay any principal of a loan in dollars of reduced purchasing power.[7]

How important is this wealth redistribution between financial creditors
and debtors? Who gains and loses in terms of households, businesses, and
governments? The overall redistribution of financial wealth has been
estimated between 1946 and 1971 as "probably" close to $600 billion.[8]
An update to 1980, when inflation rates were higher, would lead to a
figure approximating $2 trillion.[9]

While that is a large and highly subjective number, the more important question is, Who won and who lost in terms of real wealth? The
above-mentioned study noted that, in general, "households have consistently been massive net creditors. The main offsetting debtor was governments, with different types of businesses accounting for the rest of net
debt."[10] Within the household sector, it is concluded that "both the very
poor and the very rich are more exposed to inflation than the middle
income groups. The very poor have few debts (no one will lend to them)

and hold what few assets they have partly in monetary forms. The rich also have relatively few debts (though for quite different reasons) and hold a substantial part of their wealth in bonds. . . . Middle income families tend to be heavily in debt (mainly to buy houses, autos, and the like) and have the bulk of their assets in such forms, together with some common stock."[11] This is consistent with the view that in terms of *income* distribution the very poor and rich tend to be losers to the middle income group.

At another level of classification, the evidence suggests that there is a real wealth transfer from older people to younger people. The elderly have few debts and "hold a relatively high proportion of their (financial) assets in fixed (nominal) value forms. . . . Young families are generally heavily in debt."[12]

Two main points need to be made in this context. First, the aggregate evidence hides a myriad of different effects for particular families, households, and persons. Much depends on the composition of any particular household's financial asset holdings and the proportion of these which are variable price assets (the indexing issue again). Second, the above quote referred to financial assets, not real assets such as housing, land, gold, paintings, etc. If the middle and upper class have a large proportion of their total assets in such form, and if inflation raises their value equal to or more than the rate of price increase (as has been true of housing—at least in some sectors of the economy—as well as gold and land), the losses due to holdings of nonindexed financial assets may be more than offset.

Thus, except in the case of the poor, both the middle and upper income classes may gain during inflation in a wealth transfer sense. The poor, not owning much in the way of real assets and having little debt, fall further behind in both a relative income and wealth sense, especially during stagflation. Yet these broad classifications of poor, middle income, and rich doubtless hide more than they reveal regarding either wealth or income redistribution. "Overall, the redistributional effects of inflation are more complex than is often suggested, requiring analysis cutting across the broad functional income groups to individuals and smaller groups with lagging incomes and substantial net creditor positions not offset by debts or large holdings of variable price assets."[13]

CONCLUSION

Several implications are evident for the type of inflation experienced in the United States since 1965. (1) Uncertainty and shortsightedness are enhanced, thus jeopardizing the expansion of the private capital stock, which will then reduce the future rate of economic growth. (2) Households are encouraged to go more into debt to purchase various consumer durables, since debtors gain and creditors lose during inflation. This lowers the household savings ratio, which recently fell to its lowest level in decades. Unless offset by higher corporate or government savings, this drop in savings reduces the flow of investible funds for business expansion. Thus, on both the demand (item 1 above) side and the supply side, real investment is adversely affected. (3) Probably the elderly, the poor, and the rich are negatively affected, but within these very broad groupings it is difficult to sort out who gains and who loses without a detailed knowledge of expenditure and specific inflation patterns, asset and income patterns, and whatever offsetting indexing or other public and private income supplements are available. (4) Despite the inability to specify exactly who wins or loses and by how much, variable but relatively high inflation is to be viewed as a kind of random perturbation reducing real incomes all around and causing socially purposeless income and weatlh redistributions.

As such, efforts to contain inflation—in the sense of reducing its annual oscillations about whatever level and in reducing the general level —deserve to have high priority in any overall economic policy recommended for the United States and indeed all countries experiencing unusually high rates of inflation. This is even more urgent because, not only does the recent inflation slow down real overall growth and provide windfall gains and losses to those persons, households and firms who do not deserve them in any meaningful sense of merit for productive efforts or punishment for economic mistakes, but there is also the ever present danger that inflation will begin to accelerate rapidly to a new and higher plateau, as it has historically done with enormous social, economic and political consequences (see chapter 2 on secular inflation). While the kind of inflation recently experienced may neither be the cruelest tax nor cause the end of capitalism (as suggested by Lenin), if it is not contained with positive evidence of reduction, the latter possibilities are always present. The really difficult question is how to do it at social costs that yield at least equivalent benefits. This is the subject of the next chapter.

7 Cures for Inflation

A BRIEF REVIEW

The previous chapter has argued that the attempt to cure inflation is worth considerable effort and some sacrifice. Curing inflation does not mean reducing the rate of growth of the CPI or GNP deflator to zero, for reasons noted earlier in connection with deficiencies in either price index and especially the CPI. Rather, "curing inflation" means reducing the annual rates of fluctuation in either index and attempting to lower the rates to a level consistent with our experience during the 1950s and early 1960s, or at least to levels below or consistent with our major trading partners such as Canada, Western Europe, and Japan.

Chapters 3, 4, and 5 outlined the major apparent causes of inflation. Briefly they are as follows:

1. Excessive demand relative to the economy's capacity to produce. This situation, in turn, is often caused or exacerbated by excessive fiscal and/or monetary stimulus. The variability of the rate of inflation is caused in part by too great a variation in either fiscal or monetary policies—the "stop/go" problem of the late 1960s and 1970s. At the same time, of course, total private domestic spending on consumption and investment or foreign spending for U.S. exports may be excessive when combined with even regular or normal public expenditures. Monetary and fiscal policies in such instances "cause" inflation only to the extent that they accommodate the excess demand or fail to restrain it. It is the level of *total* spending relative to capacity that constitutes "demand-pull" inflation, whose origins may be either public or private.

2. The built-in downward wage and price rigidity of the economy, such that most wages and prices are much freer to rise than to fall, thereby inculcating a basic inflationary bias and contributing to stagflation. The cost-push and demand-shift explanations of inflation are based in part on this phenomenon.

3. A series of federal government policies or programs that reinforce the above, such as price supports for specific industries, minimum wage

laws, usury laws (e.g., Reg. Q), economic regulation, and so on.

4. Increasing world economic interdependence amid real or apparent relative scarcity of strategic natural resources in finite supply, such as oil.

5. Inflationary expectations generated in any economy having experienced higher than normal rates of price increase for a succession of time periods. Thus inflation tends to feed on itself along the lines of a wage-price spiral. However initiated, persistently higher-than-usual rates of inflation generate higher inflation expectations.

6. Large balance of trade and payments deficits emerging when one nation's prices of traded goods and services rise faster than those of other nations. This development often leads to currency devaluation, thereby raising the prices (costs) of imports, which, if not sharply curtailed, raises the level of domestic prices and costs.

7. Disappearance of the status quo. As various groups in society jostle for a bigger share of a more slowly increasing real income, upward pressure on the price level is bound to occur.

Some of these suggest more or less specific approaches to resolution of the present inflation problem. In addition, a series of other potential remedies not directly linked to the above have been proposed. The present chapter will examine these in turn.

REMEDIES SUGGESTED BY THE CAUSES OF INFLATION

Excessive Demand

With an unemployment rate of between 7 and 8% in mid to late 1980, a capacity utilization rate in manufacturing of barely 75% (Federal Reserve Series), a sharp decline of industrial production, a drop in real GNP as of mid-1980 (since late 1979), it is clear that there is no general excess of demand at present. The recent spate of inflation is thus not demand-pull. It is more a hangover of past inflation rates and expectations of even more, bolstered by relatively high rates of growth of the money supply. (M_2 and M_3 rose at annual rates of about 10% and 9%, respectively, during June, July, and August of 1980.) Fiscal policy has turned restrictive despite the relatively high current and anticipated federal government deficits. These are in essence passive deficits due to the 1980 recession, when government receipts rose more slowly than expenditures. If the economy were at full-employment GNP, receipts would be estimated to exceed outlays. A surplus would be anticipated at current tax rates and spending levels. In part, this shift in the federal budget contributed to the sharp decline in GNP during the second quarter of 1980. The *immediate* cause was extremely high nominal interest rates associated with the Fed's announced policy of severely restricting the money supply. This led to precipitous declines in the housing and automobile industries that spread their impact unevenly over the country.

The short-run problem is thus to get better control over the monetary aggregates and to either hold fiscal policy steady or provide a mild stimulus via a tax reduction that would at least partially offset bracket creep and the rise in social security taxes.

But the longer-run problem is more important. The economy is now (last half of 1980) in at least a mild and tentative recovery. How to sustain this, accelerate real growth, and alleviate inflation is the critical problem for the 1980s.

At the very least, we can expect that monetary and fiscal policies be used more sensibly. This may be little more than a pious hope, but, as previously noted, some lessons from the past 20 years of stabilization policy efforts have been learned. Indeed, the 1976 report of the Council of Economic Advisers, normally an "activist" body, had this to say:

> The difficult inflationary period through which we have come makes it likely that overly expansionary policies, which risk increasing inflationary pressures, will quickly influence consumers' and producers' expectations. It is a harsh fact of economic life that expectations of inflation are built into labor and other contracts in such a way as to be partly self-fulfilling. Moreover, increased inflationary expectations could restrain both consumption and investment expenditures and thus jeopardize long-term economic goals. High and variable rates of inflation not only create imbalances and sectoral distortions . . . but also raise risk premiums in investment decisions and wage bargains. . . . Policies that are perceived to entail higher inflation risks may not, therefore, affect economic activity and employment in a way that would normally be expected.
>
> There is a lesson to be drawn from past policy mistakes. The history of monetary and fiscal policies demonstrates that we have a great deal to learn about implementing discretionary policy changes. . . .
>
> The proper conclusion is not that we should forswear the use of discretionary policy. Some external shocks to the economic system can and should be offset. Furthermore, . . . occasional discretionary adjustments of the income tax schedules are called for in order to prevent excessive growth in Federal taxes. In fact, these changes may have to be more frequent if the rate of inflation continues at a somewhat higher average level than at comparable levels of economic activity in the past. Thus, discretionary policies do have an important function in our economic system. But we must be mindful of the great difficulties in successfully executing countercyclical policies.[1]

The belief in fine tuning is a thing of the past. While short-run policy shifts can be expected from time to time, the main policy thrust is aimed at the future. Reindustrialization, raising productivity and savings, stimulating research and development, developing alternative energy sources now command the attention of policymakers. All of these take time, five to ten years or more, before tangible results can be expected. In the meantime, we may expect, and indeed recommend, that monetary and fiscal policies should remain steadier than in the past. To the extent that the federal government has added to instability in the past, this should be reversed in the future.

This is, of course, far easier said than done. The political pressures to respond to every rise in the unemployment and/or inflation rate are hard to resist. It is always easier and more expedient to give something (i.e., lower taxes, increase the money supply) than to take something away (i.e., raise taxes, reduce the money supply). Furthermore, elected officials find it hard to resist "doing something" to correct perceived ills. But regardless of the specific policies proposed or enacted in response to particular events, a key difficulty is the credibility of the actions. This ultimately reduces to a generalized faith or belief that the federal government—and especially the president—knows what it or he is doing. Such faith is now, understandably, at an all-time low, at least since World War II. The uncertainties in the situation confronting all countries in the Western world (and everywhere else), combined with a reduced power and ability of the United States to respond, compound the problem. It is difficult for even an overwhelmingly popular president to know either what to do or how to do it.

The fact is that in economic affairs, as in all others, the uncertainties are so confusing that unless there is a problem of massive dimensions, such as unemployment over 10% or inflation over 15% for a sustained period (say, two calendar quarters), the appropriate strategy in terms of monetary or fiscal policy is far from obvious. That politicians elected for relatively short terms will try to "do something" is axiomatic. President Nixon tried to "hang in there" with his ill-fated "game plan" but was finally induced to yield to wage-price controls. A strong president, with a large mandate, is therefore essential to withstand a succession of "quick fixes" that may have singularly undesirable long-run consequences.

The present prospects are bleak in this respect, although Mr. Reagan's large mandate is promising. In addition, the Congress, as is evident by the recent report of the Joint Economic Committee, may be able to enforce a steadier set of monetary and fiscal policies and prevent the mistakes of the past twenty years. Steadiness may be all the more important in view of the apparent rapid growth of the "underground economy" alluded to in chapter 4. Recent estimates of unrecorded activity put it in the range of over one-fifth of recorded GNP. This could mean that inflation and unemployment are seriously overstated and that productivity is understated. What appears as a serious situation in each of these areas may not in fact be the case and thus not require any policy response. The underground economy may not only be large but recent estimates suggest that it is growing very rapidly. In this economy, prices are lower[2] (due to no taxation), employment obviously higher, and, possibly, productivity greater. Thus, the economy may be better than the observed statistics indicate. "The economic patient is much healthier than we imagine. The trouble is that the thermometer by which the economy's health is judged has gone awry."[3]

The apparently increasing unreliability of the data used to monitor the economy clearly calls for more steadiness in terms of response as well as for efforts to improve the evidence.

Downward Wage and Price Flexibility

It is not at all clear that downward flexibility of money wages is either desirable, even in a strict economic sense, or feasible from a policy point of view. It may not be desirable as an attempt to cure unemployment, because a reduction in the money wage rate may simply reduce total labor income. Since the latter accounts for about 70% of total national income, it represents the greatest source of overall purchasing power. A reduction of wages may reduce total spending in the economy and thus cause *more* unemployment, rather than reduce it.

A wage rate reduction would, however, reduce unit production costs and, with stable prices, lead to higher profits and thus to more investment. However, if the lower wage rate also reduced total demand, any stimulus to investment would be offset, possibly completely or more or less than completely. With stable prices and falling money wages, the real purchasing power of the largest single group in society, the labor force, would decline. The social, political, as well as economic consequences of this would doubtless be disastrous. Certainly in democratic societies, there has always been a reluctance to treat the buying and selling of labor in the same manner as peanuts, wheat, or coffee. Wage rate changes on a pervasive scale directly affect the incomes of the vast majority of the population, unlike a change in the price of peanuts. Therefore, living standards are directly affected by wage changes to an extent far more significant than by changes in particular commodity prices. As the Clayton Act put it in 1914, "the labor of a human being is not an article or commodity of commerce."

There is enormous uncertainty in all of the relationships between money wage changes, unemployment rates, and inflation. Certainly, lower money wages would help alleviate inflation. However, the short-run consequences appear to be so severe that few recommend any absolute reduction in money wages. Real wages can, and have, fallen as money wages lag behind prices. But any attempt to reduce both money and real wages would be viewed as a conspiracy of the rich against the poor.

Nor is there any way, short of massive unemployment, whereby the federal government could engineer a general reduction of money wages. At most, governments recommend, cajole, and beg for "money wage restraint." That is, they seek to limit the increase in money wages to the gains in output per man-hour (i.e., productivity). In this way, unit labor costs remain constant, which helps to stabilize the overall price level. However, with high inflation expectations and downward inflexibility of many prices, the labor force correctly views even this policy of wage restraint as forcing the burden of the anti-inflation fight totally on labor. Naturally, such policies will be resisted, often violently.

The only rational conclusion is that money wage rate *reductions* cannot and should not attempt to be engineered by the federal government as part of any anti-inflation policy. Specific workers in specific companies may voluntarily agree to some wage reduction, as has happened occasionally to prevent the firm's bankruptcy.[4] But as an overall policy, downward wage flexibility has little to recommend it.

On the other hand, downward flexibility of the prices of the goods and services we buy is essential for the working of the market system. Prices and profit prospects are the signals that guide resource flows from one sector of the economy to another. It is likewise the prices of goods and services that constitute our several price indexes. By definition, then, enhanced downward price flexibility is essential if any of the overall price indexes are ever to fall. Even slowing their general rate of increase to levels below, say, 5% will require that in some major sectors of the economy prices can fall or at least stabilize. In addition, greater downward price flexibility is essential to tackle the stagflation problem as noted in chapter 3.

How can we encourage price reductions and/or restrain price increases?

1. We can stimulate competition. This can be done by more vigorous antitrust enforcement—by opening up hitherto protected industries to additional rivals (as is now happening or has happened with respect to communications and transportation), by changing the entry provisions of regulated industries (i.e., deregulating in whole or in part), and by reducing the protection of domestic industries from foreign competition. These actions would reduce the extent of concentration of economic power and provide powerful incentives to compete on a price as well as quality basis.

Yet each of these separate initiatives will evoke strong negative reactions because each has important short-term adverse impacts. For example, more vigorous antitrust policies may adversely affect business confidence and hence reduce much needed private investment at the very time we are counting on this investment to accelerate the recovery of late 1980 and improve productivity during the 1980s. The opening of certain areas of domestic communication was successfully opposed by the Bell System for decades. The deregulation of civil aviation in 1977, of trucks and railroads in 1980, took almost twenty years of effort due to vigorous opposition to change by both the companies and unions affected. Nor has there been much evidence that air fares have declined except on specific highly competitive routes. On the contrary, overall air fares are now much higher than before deregulation. To be sure, one can argue that without deregulation they would have been even higher and that now travellers have a wider mix of fare/quality alternatives. But this is scarcely convincing to a skeptical public. The rail deregulation bill passed in October 1980 was explicitly designed to provide railroads with a chance to increase their revenues by selective rate *increases*, with a view to making them not only financially viable but able to improve track, service, and overall service quality. Again, a skeptical public will not readily be convinced that, *over time*, this will provide more efficient service at lower cost than subsidy or outright nationalization. The short-run effects will be to raise fares and rates—scarcely a self-evident cure for inflation.

Finally, permitting—nay, encouraging—foreign competition, in the face of excessive levels of domestic unemployment, is not something to be attempted lightly. Already the steel, auto, and TV industries (among others) have sought protection against imports with strong union support. Yet increased competition from whatever source is the best protection from ever-increasing prices and provides incentives for domestic producers to improve efficiency and quality at competitive prices. The short-run impact is, however, deemed singularly undesirable in terms of domestic output and employment.

2. Downward price movement is further prevented or hindered by sales and excise taxes and by the employer share of social security taxes. The latter, in particular, have risen sharply over the last several years, and further increases have already been scheduled. Sales and excise taxes result directly in higher purchase prices, and the social security taxes are shifted forward into higher prices. The added costs of pollution, health, safety, and discrimination controls have similar effects, as do price support programs, mainly in agriculture and the minimum wage law.

Thus, a shift in taxation away from sales or excise taxes toward direct income taxation would tend to make a contribution to lower prices in a once-and-for-all sense. But most sales taxes are imposed at the state and local level. It has therefore been suggested that the federal government, in exchange for reductions in such state and local taxes, should provide a payment equivalent to revenues foregone. This may lead to larger federal deficits, themselves inflationary if the economy is close to capacity.

Again, there are trade-offs with respect to the other items noted above. We cannot and should not abandon the efforts to improve the environment, health, safety, and so on. But, as argued in chapter 4, many of the present efforts are not cost-effective. A more careful balancing of the costs relative to benefits would contribute, albeit marginally, to lower costs and hence lower prices, especially in a more competitive milieu.

Price support programs and minimum wage laws are equally controversial, as would be their modification. Yet reduction in support levels or prevention of further increases would make a marginal contribution to an anti-inflationary policy. In terms of political controversy, however, the gains may not come close to the costs.

It is easier to devise, but not to execute, policies designed to limit wages and prices. These require some criteria of "acceptable" wage and price increases or, as they are usually called, "wage and price guidelines." These will be discussed further below. Suffice it to say here that, given such guidelines and some enforcement powers, it is possible to limit some wage and price increases. One approach to this limiting is often referred to as a "tax based incomes policy" or TIPS, of which more later. It is not, however, so much designed to promote downward wage or price flexibility as to limit or inhibit excessive upward flexibility. The same is true of wage and price controls.

3. Not much can or should be done about increasing world economic

interdependence. The inflationary consequences of continued upward boosts in oil prices have already been noted both in terms of higher domestic costs, balance of payments deficits, and the associated downward pressure on the dollar. The desirability of searching for more domestic oil and gas as well as for alternative energy sources is apparent. The payoff will, of course, take many years and indeed will preoccupy us during the 1980s. In the short run, decontrol of prices as presently envisaged will accentuate inflation. But if this encourages the appropriate supply-side responses, the real cost should eventually subside along with the pressure on the dollar. Again, this constitutes a trade-off between short-run increases in inflationary pressures and long-run deflationary pressures.

4. The reversal of inflationary expectations requires some evidence that the inflation rate is decreasing and that the monetary and fiscal policies will persevere even in the face of rising unemployment. But is it worth it? Some plausible estimates suggest that every one percent reduction in the basic inflation rate "costs" something like 10% of one year's GNP, or about $250 billion at present levels of nominal GNP.[5] Once again, there is an apparent short-run trade-off.

Inflation expectations may be lowered by such policy pronouncements as the Fed's declaration in October 1980 that the rate of growth of the money supply would henceforth be contained within a substantially lower range. This only works if there is substantial credibility and evidence that the Fed can and will try to stabilize monetary growth. For a while, the Fed's policy seemed to work—the inflation rate dropped sharply, as did interest rates. It was widely believed that inflation expectations had been revised downwards. Yet this coincided with the steep contraction of GNP in the second quarter of 1980. Since then, the Fed's performance has been erratic. It appears that inflation expectations have been revised upwards once again. The widely anticipated increase in the federal deficit, even though a passive deficit, reinforces this.

A final alternative approach to revising expectations downward is wage and price controls. Certainly, this was one of the purposes of the first wage-price freeze of the Nixon administration. This alternative, too, has numerous undesirable side effects,[6] not the least of which was its failure to work in any permanent sense.

MORE DRASTIC "REMEDIES"

The foregoing possible courses of action are suggested by the factors causing or contributing to inflationary pressures previously enumerated above. Most of them are relatively modest and their results uncertain. The uncertainty arises not only because of lack of knowledge of their relationship to the specific causal or contributing factor they are directed at, but also because the relative importance of each such factor is unknown. In addition, there are various economic side effects and trade-offs whose consequences may be more adverse than whatever deflationary effects they may have.

In addition to these so-called remedies (or, better, approaches to the inflation problem), three so-called classic approaches have often been suggested and frequently tried in the United States or other countries. These are indexation, wage-price guidelines, and wage-price controls. Each will be discussed in turn.

Indexation

As noted in the discussion of Brazilian inflation in chapter 2, indexation is the linking of specified incomes, taxes, or assets, denominated in nominal terms (i.e., so many dollars per period), to the rate of inflation, actual, anticipated, or past. For example, assume a wage contract is signed paying $1,000 per period, but subject to an indexation clause permitting a full adjustment for inflation. If the inflation rate were zero during the period, workers would receive $1,000 per period. But if the price level rose 5% during the period, the monetary payment would be $1050, thus maintaining the "real" wage ($\frac{\$1050}{1.05} = \$1,000$). Similarly, on a loan for $1,000, a borrower may have to repay $1050 if prices are stable during the period, or $1155 if prices rose by 10%, to preserve the real purchasing power of $1050 (since $1155 is 110% of $1050).

Indexation is thus an attempt to prevent many of the income and wealth redistributions associated with unanticipated inflation. It is less an attempt to cure inflation than to moderate its impact. Social security payments in the United States are indexed, and in many industries the wage rate is indexed at least partially. The latter is referred to as cost-of-living adjustments for unanticipated inflation during the period of the contract. If inflation were correctly anticipated, the wage bargain would automatically include an inflation-related nominal income component, and no indexation would be necessary.

In practice, it is not possible to index all incomes and asset values. Nor is it clear which of the several price indexes should be used to raise nominal payments or values. The CPI is almost exclusively used in the United States even though it is something of a flawed indicator. The frequency of adjustment of nominal values also needs to be specified. If adjustments are not made at the same time for all incomes and assets, serious problems may emerge. In Brazil, for example, the assets of the Housing Finance System were not adjusted for inflation as rapidly as its liabilities, causing short-run balance sheet anomalies.[7] Any persons or organizations whose incomes were indexed more slowly than expenses would suffer a chronic cash flow problem and vice versa.

Thus, unless indexation can be made to apply to at least most incomes and/or assets using the same price index with the same time lag for adjustment (yearly or quarterly) and on the same basis (ex post or ex ante), some income and asset redistribution will occur. Such a pervasive and uniform system of indexation has never been attempted. It is doubtful that such a system could or should even be attempted for a variety of reasons. For example, the value of many assets is determined by the incomes or yields they produce. Indexing both assets and incomes can therefore yield some significant distortions and inconsistencies.[8] This is especially important in the case of home mortgages and the issue of variable-rate mortgages. The latter in essence indexes (partially) the interest but not the principal of the home loan. Indeed, both principal and interest cannot be indexed. When the interest is indexed, the lender is somewhat protected from the risks of inflation, but this indexation creates new risks for the borrowers. Conversely, if the principal is indexed, the borrower would pay proportionately higher monthly nominal amounts, but these would be offset by the higher value of the property represented by the loan and, presumably, by the home owner's higher income due to rising inflation rates.[9] The problem of income versus asset indexing thus involves a shift in risks between borrowers and lenders.

One area of indexation, however, would help eliminate the "tax bracket creep" associated with inflation. This involves indexing the tax system so that tax brackets would increase in proportion to the price level. Such a practice would leave the level of *real* taxes invariant with respect to nominal incomes. For example, if income initially were $20,000, income taxes $8,000, after-tax income would be $12,000. Suppose the price level doubled. Nominal income would then be $40,000 if this individual's *real* income (i.e., its purchasing power) were to remain the same. Yet a progressive tax system based on nominal income, as in the United States and most other Western countries, would take proportionately more of a $40,000 income than from a $20,000 income. Assume the tax paid on $40,000 were not $16,000, as it would be under a proportional tax system, but $25,000. Nominal, after-tax income would be $15,000 but the purchasing power of $15,000 would be cut in half. Real, after-tax income would then fall from $12,000 to $7,500. With an indexed tax system, the doubling of nominal income would lead to only a doubling of taxes and hence a maintenance of real, after-tax income.

To the extent that bracket creep is both beneficial to the government and detrimental to incentives, it reduces the federal government's concern with inflation and may encourage more public spending. At the same time, it may reduce overall productivity and stimulate the underground economy. The combined effect is likely to exacerbate measured inflation. Indexation of tax brackets, exemptions, or other aspects of the tax system would temper the probable inflationary stimulus provided by bracket creep. Indexing of business taxes, to avoid unlegislated increases due to inflation, would stimulate investment and innovation. "When inflation increases from zero to 10%, a corporation that had been earning 10% on its capital might need as much as 20% to give it an equivalent profit. Under present law, however, the corporation would then pay twice as much tax on earnings whose purchasing power had not increased."[10]

On the other hand, indexation would reduce the automatic stabilization properties of a progressive tax system based on nominal incomes. Once again, there are obvious trade-offs in indexation and different winners and losers, whose net impact on inflation, unemployment, and growth is difficult to disentangle.

In general, the case for indexation is that it prevents *some* of the distortions in income and wealth distribution caused by inflation (see chapter 6). Full indexing of pension-type incomes, as is done with social security and some pension plans, would alleviate the misery of many of our older citizens. But there are serious problems with indexation. We have already noted some difficulties with respect to which incomes, assets, or taxes to index, which price index to use, and the frequency with which such incomes or assets are indexed. These are mostly pragmatic problems that, in principle at least, can be overcome.

Yet there are more substantive reasons for not relying on an extensive system of indexation. Indexation speeds the response to inflationary disturbances. Thus, an initial supply-side shock, as in the case of oil prices (which might otherwise be only a one-shot increase in, say, the CPI or GNP deflator), becomes fully embedded in a sequence of upward wage and price adjustments from which there is no subsequent reduction. This reinforces the downward wage and price inflexibility of the economy as a whole. It may also exacerbate inflation if the Fed validates the increase in the price level by raising the money supply.

Extensive indexing enables people to adapt more easily and quickly to inflationary forces. It therefore may reduce the resolve to attempt to prevent inflation, which in fact has serious macroeconomic consequences over and above the redistributive impacts noted earlier (chapter 6).

On balance, some increased indexation will doubtless occur if inflationary pressures continue as they likely will. But in the interests of overall stability and growth, indexing should be limited to those areas where its absence creates serious disturbances or inequities, not where it is relatively easy to adapt.

Even so, since the CPI relates to a fixed market basket of goods and services, indexing of all incomes (say wages) will affect individuals differently if their proportional purchases of the various goods and services differ markedly from the national average. There is indeed no way of eliminating *all* inequitable income or asset redistributions. Widespread indexation is in essence an admission of defeat in the inflation battle and, for this and the other reasons noted above, should only be selectively and carefully encouraged.

Wage and Price Guidelines

Indexation is something of a palliative, an attempt to preserve *real* values in the face of rapidly shifting nominal values. It does not therefore represent an attack on the evil itself. A somewhat more positive approach to inflation is the institution of wage and price guidelines.

Wage and price guidelines involve the federal government setting permissible or voluntary percentage increases in wages and prices, usually on an annual basis. Thus the government may specify that wages should increase by no more than 7% and prices no more than, say, 5%. The differences between the two are presumed to reflect the increase in labor productivity. If there is general compliance, prices should rise by about 5%, and thus real wages would increase by 2%—a rise equivalent to the increase in productivity. In this way, inflation may be contained although not eliminated. Ideally, of course, one could set the guidelines for wages at precisely the increase in labor productivity (output per man-hour). This would keep unit labor costs constant and, other things being equal, could stabilize the overall price level.

The wage-price guidelines were first enunciated in the 1962 *Annual Report of the Council of Economic Advisers*. Recognizing that in many industries "private parties may exercise considerable discretion over the terms of wage bargains and price decisions," the Council argued that such discretion ought to recognize the "public interest" in such decisions. In other words, the council viewed much of the then existing inflation as cost-push and sought to induce large firms and unions to behave as if they were subject to impersonal market forces and a high degree of competitive pressure. Not being subject to such pressures implied the need for some supplemental "pressures" or considerations, as implied in the guidelines. Mandatory restraints were not then deemed desirable on the grounds that they would permit undue federal influence in collective bargaining and private pricing decisions. Nor were mandatory wage and price controls, rather than voluntary guidelines, deemed feasible in a "diffuse and decentralized continental economy."[11]

The Council recognized that the national averages concerning productivity were not relevant to specific industries and thus enunciated the following:

> The general guide for noninflationary wage behavior is that the rate of increase in wage rates (including fringe benefits) in each industry be equal to the trend rate of over-all productivity increase. General acceptance of this guide would maintain stability of labor cost per unit of output for the economy as a whole—though not, of course, for individual industries.
>
> The general guide for non-inflationary price behavior calls for price reductions if the industry's rate of productivity increase exceeds the over-all rate—for this would mean declining unit labor costs; it calls for an increase in price if the opposite prevails; and it calls for stable prices if the two rates of productivity increase are equal.[12]

Wage and price guidelines have since been attempted, most recently under the aegis of the Council on Wage and Price Stability (see chapter 4, "Introduction"). However, their usefulness as a device to temper inflationary forces is limited. In the first place, they are voluntary. No firm or union is legally bound to them by any constraint such as fines for noncompliance. To be sure, certain stimuli to "voluntary" compliance can be invoked: measures such as "jawboning," refusal of the government to purchase from firms violating the guidelines, public censure of such firms or unions, threats of antitrust action, tariff reduction, or accelerated sales of commodities from government stockpiles relevant to noncomplying industries. These are in essence selected "clubs in the closet" that may induce certain industries and unions to "voluntarily" comply.

Yet these are terribly messy and highly selective approaches to overall inflationary pressures. Special circumstances in particular industries may well justify deviations from the guidelines. However, such deviations may also be sanctioned on grounds other than efficiency or their inflationary impacts, such as political gain (the industry involved may have contributed substantially to the president's election or reelection campaign). The singling out of a particular firm or union for either sanctions or exemptions from the guidelines is thus subject to all the problems of favoritism, nepotism, bribery, or corruption. Nor is the data on industry productivity trends sufficiently unambiguous to warrant any rigid application of the guidelines. Some industries may have lagged behind past cost increases and thus really need a catchup above the norm. Some industries may need to offer higher wage increases to attract labor. These and other difficulties were early recognized. But the number of exceptional cases steadily mounts.

The evidence suggests that guidelines had some effect, albeit mild, until about 1966. Thereafter, with the burgeoning demand-pull or excess demand inflation associated with the Indochina wars, they ceased to be effective. There is no evidence that their revival under President Carter made any impact whatsoever in the war against inflation. Indeed, one of the clubs in the closet, refusal of the government to purchase from a noncomplying firm, was explicitly declared to be unconstitutional by the Supreme Court. The exhortation to big business and labor not to take advantage of monopolistic position with regard to prices and wages in specific industries cannot be very effective, given the rates of inflation experienced since the late 1960s. Nor can they do much more than temporarily restrain persistent market forces working in the opposite direction.

Frustration over the apparently increasingly severe trade-offs between inflation and unemployment (as evident by the shifting Phillips curve) as well as the impotence of monetary and fiscal policies to alleviate inflation at acceptable costs in terms of unemployment and output foregone, leads rather naturally to a policy of mandatory wage and price controls.

Short of this rather Draconian, last-ditch effort, however, further suggestions have been made to rescue "voluntarism." These involve providing incentives to firms and workers who remain within preset guidelines or specific monetary penalties for violators. Such policies are referred to as "tax-based incomes policies" or TIPS. In the incentive version, all firms and workers staying within the guidelines would receive a tax rebate of some predetermined amount. In the penalty version, firms and workers raising prices and wages above the guidelines would incur a penalty tax on the excess.

One advantage of such a system is that firms and workers can voluntarily exceed or stay within the guidelines at some known penalty or reward. In addition, management has an extra bargaining tool for inducing wage restraint: hence, knowing that wage excesses will be taxed or that wages below the guidelines will be rewarded by tax relief to the workers, management can more effectively bargain for smaller wage increases. There are thus real advantages over either wage-price guidelines, with unknown or unpredictable sanctions and rewards, or wage-price controls, with little scope for flexibility.

Yet there are serious problems with regard to TIPS. Collective bargaining agreements involve far more than nominal wages. They also involve fringe benefits such as vacations, pension and hospitalization benefits, rewards based on length of service, promotion procedures, and so on. A high tax on wage excesses may simply lead to cost-increasing concessions on the fringes. This could protract bargaining sessions and/or lead to more strike activity.

If the guideline is set too high, TIPS have no effect. If too low, adverse labor reaction with increased potential strike activity will result. Since the aim is to set a guideline that permits wages to rise consistent with increased productivity, a single, overall guideline fails to account for inter-industry or inter-firm differences in productivity. As noted earlier, such productivity trends are difficult to establish unambiguously.

Monitoring the thousands of wage and price adjustments that occur constantly in the economy creates enormous administrative and empirical difficulties. These problems necessitate the application of TIPS to a manageable group of large industries. But which ones to include or exclude is not something amenable to easy or precise solution. How to deal with firms that previously negotiated cost-of-living escalators over a lengthy period is yet another problem.

While reasonable though inherently arbitrary resolution of these and other matters can be made, the costs may not begin to exceed the benefits. Nor is there any assurance that the inflationary pressures of the 1970s were largely of the wage-push variety as is implicit in TIPS.

Such a policy has not yet been attempted in the United States. Indeed, it may raise serious legal and constitutional problems that need to be resolved first. The Carter Administration was widely reported to have discussed TIPS, earlier rejected it, and then, in the campaign of 1980, promised to reconsider it should Mr. Carter be reelected. The point is now moot.

Wage and Price Controls

Abandoning even a reinforced "voluntarism," the final solution often reverted to by governments here and elsewhere is mandatory wage and price controls. These controls take the form of either temporary freezes of wages and prices, such as the 90-day freeze imposed on 15 August 1971 as part of President Nixon's "New Economic Policy" or statutory ceilings on price and wage increases. Not all prices and wages are or can be subjected to such freezes or ceilings. Usually, agricultural products are exempted, while export and import prices cannot be controlled.

In the present context, there is, according to various public opinion polls, a mild preference for such controls. We need therefore to examine some of the reasons for them, determine their good and bad effects, and then draw some conclusions. There is no unanimity of opinion in the economics profession concerning either their desirability or their inevitability. The following sections seek to sort out their pros and cons.

The Reasons for Mandatory Controls

Mandatory controls are almost invariably imposed during wartime, at least during any major war. The resulting massive shifts of resources from civilian to military production leads to extremely high prices of consumer goods. Ceiling prices, combined with rationing of necessities, are deemed essential to prevent severe distortions. War is inherently inflationary since incomes are generated for activity that produces no output increase available for civilians to buy. Increased demands are thus focused on a shrinking supply in the consumer goods sector. The need for such controls and an equitable rationing system is self-evident in a major war such as World War II. Yet even given widespread support and compliance during that war, black markets grew up. The longer the controls existed, the greater became the evasions and needed adjustments in the price level.

During peacetime, controls do not have the sort of voluntary acceptance and compliance associated with the war effort. Their rationale is far less compelling. This implies that peacetime controls are workable only for relatively short periods and that their enforcement is less effective and more burdensome.

One of the reasons suggested for peacetime controls by those seeking to impose them is to give the government a certain "breathing space" to think through alternative anti-inflationary strategies. Less charitably, these controls are imposed because the government doesn't know what else to do. The necessity to "do something" is omnipresent in the face of unacceptably high rates of inflation. If restraining aggregate demand merely causes more unemployment and reduced output without much effect on inflation, then controls may give a sense of comfort to both the public at large and the administration. Yet they are really a symptom of failure—"nothing else seems to work so let us try controls," is the implicit assumption.

Somewhat more substantively, controls seek to break inflation expectations. To the extent that they succeed, the rate of inflation in the post-control period should be lower than what otherwise would have occurred. As the Council put it in their 1972 Report, "The basic premise of the price-wage controls system is that the inflation of 1970 and 1971 was the result of expectations, contracts, and patterns of behavior built up during the earlier period, beginning in 1965, when there was an inflationary excess of demand."[13] Arnold Weber, director of the then Cost-of-Living Council which administered the 90-day freeze, stipulated that one of the "primary objectives of the overall program was to dissipate inflationary expectations."[14]

Controls, of course, prevent the price system from performing its resource allocative functions. Those advocating controls therefore justify them on the grounds that the allocative function is not being performed very well in the large, non-price-competitive section of the U.S. economy. The concentrated sectors of the economy are viewed as pushing up prices and wages exorbitantly and preventing downward wage-price flexibility (the cost-push, demand-shift explanations of inflation). Since antitrust policy is relatively ineffective in restraining price and wage increases on a national scale, a broader set of "controls" is necessary.

These rationalizations have frequently been given, and they are not without some merit. Clearly, the public feels more comfortable knowing that their elected representatives are not sitting idly by and allowing inflation to continue along its devastating course. Similarly, if expectations can be revised downward by controls, they may prove to be of longer term benefit. Yet to revise them downward requires a belief that controls will work, that they will not merely suppress inflation for a short time after which inflationary forces will burgeon once again. Without such faith and widespread willingness to comply, expectations will not be revised. Removal of controls will trigger a fresh outburst of inflation as, in fact, did occur. Reimposition of controls then becomes self-defeating. Both business and labor perceive that controls are ineffective. Thus prices are pushed up promptly upon their removal, perhaps higher than would otherwise have happened. During the decontrol period, prices and wages will not fall, since no one wants to be caught with his prices (wages) down in the next freeze. A succession of price controls as typified the early 1970s (three freezes within a three-year period) merely reinforces the already substantial downward price and wage rigidity of the economy.

Finally, the concentrated industries argument, appealing to many, cannot explain the inflationary *process*. There is no evidence that either monopoly power or concentration increased rapidly in the early 1970s following the demand-pull inflation of the late 1960s. Concentration does inhibit downward price flexibility but by itself cannot account for the inflation of the 1970s.

Thus, the usual reasons advanced for mandatory wage-price controls are at best convenient rationalizations of the failure of other policy initiatives, except in the case of a major increase in military expenditures. Wage-price controls can be somewhat effective for a short period of time but seldom leave any enduring positive effect. This may not be all bad. The economy, after all, survived World War II. The controls—plus rationing, forced saving, exhortations to conserve for the war effort, and widespread belief that they were essential and reasonably equitable— were among the costs of survival. In peacetime, there are few of these reinforcing factors: hence, the probability of a successful longer-run attack on inflation through controls is low indeed. The experience of the early 1970s has seriously reduced this probability even further. Indeed, the expectation of future controls, even in a Reagan Administration, powerfully reinforces downward price rigidity.

Costs of Controls

A huge administrative staff is required to implement, monitor, and make reasonable exceptions to the wage and price ceilings actually established. The longer the controls are in effect, the greater the number of needed exceptions. Indeed, almost every wage and price frozen becomes a candidate for exceptions at one time or another. Many argue that the freeze caught them at an inopportune moment, thereby necessitating adjustments under the threat of bankruptcy. Since not all prices are or can be controlled (e.g., import and export prices), specific firms can argue for at least such cost "pass throughs." If these occur, costs for purchasers of such products will rise, and they can argue for the same treatment. Prices in the United States for some products lower than in overseas markets will induce exports, thereby shrinking domestic supplies and generating severe upward price pressures. Such pressures require either higher allowable domestic prices or restrictions on exports. Just prior to the final removal of controls in 1974, the following industries had been exempted for a variety of reasons: fertilizer, cement, zinc, aluminum, automobiles, mobile homes, rubber tires and tubes, all retail trade, furniture, paper, coal, shoes and other footwear, canned fruits and vegetables, petrochemicals, prepared foods, and semiconductors.

Decisions on all of these exemptions must be made, which requires a large staff. The controls in 1971–73 required a staff of over 4,000. But there are also serious costs to businesses and labor as they seek to comply with all of the standards or request exemption. In addition, there are the costs of productive effort foregone as various firms and workers seek to evade the controls. Black marketeering also absorbs resources that might otherwise be used to produce output of needed goods and services. To be fair and equitable, mandatory controls would have to be comprehensive, covering not only wages and prices but also interest rates, rents, and profits, with all of their attendant problems requiring a small army to administer and enforce.

Misallocation of resources also occurs as prices no longer fulfill their role of guiding resources in conformity with consumers' tastes and preferences. Some of these distortions may be quite severe. For example, during the 60-day freeze imposed in mid-1973, "uncontrolled feed grain prices rose sharply. But since meat prices were frozen, production of livestock and poultry became unprofitable. Farmers slaughtered livestock and poultry rather than market them."[15] With the increasing number of exemptions, further distortions of this ilk become inevitable.

Other "costs" include the reduction in freedom of economic choice. The government becomes a partner in every major economic negotiation. The market system becomes increasingly subservient to rules, regulations, and exceptions determined by persons remote from the operating environment. Evasion becomes more pervasive over time as quality of products is diluted at the fixed price or the underground economy grows.

These and other costs constitute a rather severe indictment of controls. Yet very thoughtful people have argued for them. Clearly, controls offer some real or potential benefits other than those of a placebo nature.

Benefits of Controls

The controls of President Truman in the Korean war appeared to "work." There is some, albeit weak, evidence that the controls in the early 1970s reduced the inflation rate somewhat during the period of controls. This finding is by no means uncontested but is certainly plausible. The so-called failure of these controls may be attributable to bad luck or administration by people who basically disliked them. Perhaps, like Christianity, they have not really been tried. The bad luck included, of course, the OPEC price increases, the worldwide crop shortfalls, excessive demand stimulus domestically, a worldwide boom in 1973, and an administration increasingly handicapped by Watergate.

It is often argued that wage-price controls are a necessary standby expedient, which, if used in conjunction with restrained monetary and fiscal policies plus the other supplementary measures noted above, *can* be effective in both temporarily containing inflation and reducing inflation expectations. The controls of the early 1970s were, it is believed, taken off before they really had a chance to work.

The verdict on controls in a benefit-cost sense cannot be definitive. Defenders and critics alike concede that they are indeed messy, costly, and inevitably somewhat inequitable. All concede that the longer they are in place, the messier they get. But the alternatives of ongoing inflation may be even messier, more costly, more inequitable. As Walter Heller put it,

> whatever the merits of an 'ideal' controls program, there would be little merit in a program that has to go it alone without the supporting fiscal-monetary restraint, is riddled with special-interest exceptions and is preceded by months of pulling, hauling and indecision. . . . (T) he process that produces the controls is as important as the controls themselves.[16]

We can ill afford to reject out-of-hand any mechanism that has prospects of solving the inflationary dilemma.

IMPLICATIONS OF THE REMEDIES

The foregoing catalog of "things that might be done" suggests that every one has some severe economic or political drawback. Nor could any one of them by itself successfully attack such a multifaceted problem. Yet a package of such activities sustained over a long enough time has some prospects of success.

But underlying all such packages of programs is the issue of productivity and what needs to be done to revive the flagging efficiency of the U.S. economy. For unless we can reverse the productivity demise, there is no possibility of either raising real output per head in the future or of reducing the basic inflation rate at acceptable costs in terms of output foregone or unemployment.

The Issue of Productivity

One key aspect of stagflation is lagging productivity. The belated rediscovery of the business cycle during the 1970s and the coexistence of higher than normal unemployment and inflation rates is underlain by sharply declining and recently negative rates of productivity growth. Until these trends are reversed, there will be no getting out of the stagflation swamp.

Evidence on Productivity

The most frequently used indicator of productivity is output per hour of the private business sector. This index grew at an annual average rate of close to 3% between 1948 and 1965. From 1965 to the present, the rate fell below 2% and became negative in 1979. Because of the 1980 contraction, it will probably be negative once more because output fluctuates more rapidly than hours of work. Many observers are forecasting rates of productivity growth in the range of 1–1½% for the next four to five years. The generally poorer productivity performance of the 1970s is largely due to the reemergence of the business cycle and slow overall growth of the economy in the latter years of the decade, now fortunately over.

Broader measures of productivity—such as "total" factor productivity, which uses a weighted average of labor and capital inputs in the denominator—show a somewhat similar trend.

Trends of productivity by major branches of industry have generally declined since 1948–1965. Only the "communications" sector had a higher rate of productivity growth in the 1972–1977 period than earlier. Productivity in mining declined from +4.3% per year in the earlier period to an astonishing −5.1% per year in the middle 1970s. The construction industry's productivity fell from +3.4% (1948–1965) to −0.8% (1972–1977). Electricity, gas, and sanitary services likewise suffered a sharp decline in productivity from 6.3% per year to barely 1.0% in the latter period.[17]

International comparisons are equally dismal. Although all the major OECD countries have experienced productivity slowdowns, in the United States "this decline started earlier and has lasted longer than in other industrial economies."[18] Inadequate as much of the data are, they nevertheless all portray a rather sharp and prolonged decline of U.S. productivity, both in the aggregate and for most major sectors.

The Importance of Productivity

It is difficult to overemphasize the importance of attempting to reverse the declining rate of productivity in the United States. Virtually all macroeconomic studies attribute 50% or more of the long-run increase in real ouput in the United States and other industrial countries to productivity gains. Indeed, as Kendrick notes, "productivity accounted for all of the increase in (real income) per capita and for more than half of the increase in total output" since World War II.[19]

Rising real standards of living require higher productivity growth. Indeed, there is a very close relationship over time between average real compensation per hour in the private business sector and output per hour.

Productivity growth is also an offset to rising money costs of labor and capital. Unit labor and capital costs can remain stable if wages and interest rates increase by amounts no greater than their respective productivity growth. As is well known, such rates in money terms have accelerated sharply over the past decade for a variety of reasons. But in the face of the productivity slowdown, there is now less of an offset to burgeoning money wages than previously. As a result, so-called core inflation[20] has risen steadily from $1\frac{1}{2}\%$ per year (1960–1965) to over 7% (1973–1979) and is currently close to 9%. Unless this rate can be reduced, there is little prospect of reducing inflation much below the double-digit level in the foreseeable future. Adding to this will be further cost-side pressures (emanating from escalating energy and other raw material costs) and certain demand-side pressures, all sustained by high inflation expectations. Rates of interest in that other widely used inflation indicator, the consumer price index (CPI), will thus continue in the double-digit range or barely below it.

Causes of the Productivity Decline

A long list of causes has been offered by various observers. These include: the failure of the capital-labor ratio to grow at its historic rate of about 2.5% per year after 1973; the rapid influx into the labor force of youths and females, whose work experience and skills were generally below those of adult men; the shift of employment away from goods production toward the service sector, where productivity, though hard to measure, is traditionally believed to be low; the plethora of new non-industry-specific agencies and governmental initiatives since the 1960s, many of which have increased costs and diverted much managerial effort away from productive activities with no increase in measured output and, some would add, few nonmeasured benefits as well;[21] a deterioration of the so-called work ethic, increased worker alienation, and a decreased entrepreneurial spirit; the inflation rate, itself partly a product of the productivity demise, generates uncertainty, which jeopardizes new investment, promotes shortsightedness and, at least to date, has given rise to stop-go aggregate demand management policies, further compounding uncertainty; decrease in real expenditures for R&D and/or the diversion of R&D resources to comply with the directives of the new or non-industry-specific agencies such as EPA, FDA, OSHA, EEOC, CPSC, and others.

Other factors have been mentioned, but the foregoing appear to be the most significant—or at least the most often mentioned.

Can the Productivity Decline be Reversed?

The answer is a resounding "Yes!" But it will take a while. New capital investment can be stimulated by various forms of tax incentives, as in 1964. We have already reached the peak of labor force growth and the sharp acceleration of youths and females as a proportion of the labor force. The labor force will be increasingly experienced and skilled. The sharp reduction in labor force growth from about 2.4% per year to less than 2% as well as its changing composition will also reduce the unemployment problem. Indeed, during the 1970s, the U.S. economy did reasonably well at creating jobs, though not well enough to accommodate the burgeoning labor force.[22]

There is little that can or should be done about the shift to the services sector. After all, that is an important aspect of any postindustrial society. However, large productivity gains appear possible in many aspects of the service and non-goods-producing sectors such as health, banking, and finance. Further computerization is likely, and the increased competition engendered in the financial community by the Depository Institutions Deregulation and Monetary Control Act of 1980 should stimulate the search for greater efficiency.

There is considerable evidence that the regulatory agencies will in the future more carefully weigh the benefits against the costs imposed by their directives. This deliberation will reduce, though not eliminate, some of their productivity-reducing impacts.

In industries subject to direct, commission-type regulation (transportation, communications, finance), the trend is in the direction of eliminating those aspects of regulation that inhibited competition. Airlines, trucking, and railroads have been partially deregulated. This deregulation should not only provide improved resource allocation (and hence greater efficiency overall) but also greater downward price flexibility as competitive forces are permitted freer sway.

There is no solid evidence that the work ethic has deteriorated. Much of the antiestablishment rhetoric of the late 1960s, associated with the Indochina war, was erroneously equated with the work ethic or worker alienation. This discontent has now evaporated, in any event. We may well witness some movement toward codetermination à la Chrysler, which, combined with some better performance by OSHA and EEOC, could take much of the sting out of whatever alienation exists. We are here on pretty mushy sociological ground, but there is no reason to expect productivity to suffer any further, if indeed it has, because of either an increase of alienation or a demise of the entrepreneurial spirit. Au contraire, with investment-inducing tax cuts, whatever flagging spirits existed should be quickly eliminated and, with a rising capital-labor ratio, higher productivity and real wages should result. Nothing so "de-alienates" as higher real wages.

It is much less certain that we can get a handle on inflation before 1985, for reasons that we have already stressed. Yet, if the above positive forces leading to improved productivity do have the expected results, that in itself should serve to drive the inflation rate perhaps well below the double-digit level. In addition, we have learned some important lessons in aggregate demand management, such as quick tax cuts that go largely to augment consumption aggravate overall inflation. Both candidates for president in 1980 promised overall tax packages which would impinge more on the supply-side of the economy. The need to increase savings is now widely recognized. Monetary and fiscal policies are now not only working together more closely than over the past 20 years but appear to be "steadier," especially the monetary policy announced late last year.

The federal government can readily fund more R&D directly. Indeed, this is already happening. It can also encourage more private R&D by special tax concessions and the like.

There is a certain—perhaps naive—optimism in the trends discussed above. Yet insofar as the economy is concerned, various trends, especially demographic ones, will inexorably pull (or push) in a positive direction. Nor are appropriate policy initiatives things of mystery. Even though we cannot fully account for the productivity slowdown, we know enough to engineer its turnaround, given more steadiness and enough time. The decade of the '80s may well be referred to by future historians as the decade of the great productivity turnaround.

CONCLUSION

I have argued that the present inflationary situation in the United States and most of the Western world is a product of many factors. Its persistence since the late 1960s is due in part to the fact that many of these factors have net positive benefits—especially those that, unfortunately or not, contribute to higher costs and reduced downward price flexibility. The situation has been aggravated by a succession of "supply-side" shocks, mostly emanating from outside the United States, and some mistakes domestically with respect to monetary and fiscal policy.

The real problem of policy formation arises because there is no knowledge of the relative importance of the inflation-enhancing factors nor any reasonable estimate of the value of the trade-offs involved. One can certainly argue, as I do, that to "come to grips" with inflation (in the sense of trying to reduce the average annual rate to, say, 6%, and reduce its quarterly or annual variance to, say, 1 or 2%) requires a broadly based policy affecting both the supply and demand sides. More importantly, such a policy needs to be pursued with a high degree of consistency over time, unless any specific approach proves to be seriously counterproductive in the short run. This is the "Thatcher problem" in England. A mere catalog of contributing causes of inflation suggests the kinds of specific approaches noted in this chapter. But without knowing the relative importance of each, the trade-offs involved, or their interrelationships, any package of policies designed to contain inflation is bound to be largely judgmental and ad hoc.

Despite these ambiguities, there is room for optimism. The demographics will partly cure stagflation and assist productivity, independent of any set of policies, unless the latter are willfully perverse. The general "kinds of things" that should be done are no mystery. Their details are, of course, another matter. But as we have seen, societies do survive even hyperinflation, sometimes in altered or less desirable forms, but often for the better. I believe that inflation, as presently measured in the United States, is neither the "cruelest tax," nor does it portend the "downfall of capitalism." There are many cruelties in this world far greater than even a 20% annual increase in the CPI. Capitalism has been transformed, or has transformed itself, regularly since the late eighteenth century. Indeed, its very flexibility, linked as it has been in the West with political democracy, insures its survival—its perpetuation of a higher degree of individual choice and personal freedom than alternative systems.

Yet inflation does impose real costs on any economy, as we tried to sort out in chapter 6. There are winners and losers as well as aggregative losses. As with any phenomenon causing pain, such as the weather, it is worthwhile incurring *some* costs to alleviate the pains, but only so long as the costs of the cure are less than the benefits. This, I believe, is the basic policy dilemma facing the United States in the 1980s—are the costs worth the benefits? What is the "price" we are willing to pay to bring the rate of increase of the CPI or GNP deflator down to some more acceptable level (say 5–6%) and reduce its volatility? The inability to answer such a question in any reasonably certain or even qualitative terms is the essence of our dilemma. The problem of how to do it is less difficult, though of course not easy. With the aid of the best economic advice available anywhere, the last four administrations have grappled with this problem, and all have failed.

Recessions as a cure for inflation have proven ineffective. This is due in part to their brevity and comparative mildness. But who would argue that they should have been more prolonged and severe? This is the "cost vs. gains" problem. What else could or should have been done or not done?

It is incumbent on an author who has raised such questions at least to suggest some answers, however subjective and judgmental they may be. I therefore venture the folowing package of proposals, which, if pursued over a period of four to five years and beyond, should reduce the level and variance of inflation at acceptable costs. These are offered without further comment, since they have been discussed at length in previous chapters.

1. Monetary and fiscal policies need to work more closely together than in the past. If contractionary influences are deemed desirable, both policies should share the burden. In short, they should be consistent. But with stagflation this is difficult to achieve. In the past, monetary policy has been more inclined to fight inflation, while fiscal policy has been more concerned with unemployment. What is needed is agreement with respect to the thrust of policy (contractionary or expansionary) and an agreement with respect to specific goals of unemployment and/or inflation.

2. Monetary policy should set a target rate of growth of M_3 at a level consistent with the growth of capacity of the system, which I would estimate as at least 3% per year. A target growth rate of M_3 of between 3 and 6% would seem reasonable.

3. Fiscal policy should aim for a full-employment balanced federal budget, in which full employment is defined as an unemployment rate

of 5%. But fiscal policy should also be flexible on an annual basis to offset "tax bracket creep" and to provide incentives to investment in business plant and equipment by investment tax credit, LIFO accounting methods, and accelerated depreciation. Budget balancing as an ideology should be explicitly denied.

4. Supply-side economics should be pursued with vigor. This policy implies increased federally funded research and development expenditures plus accelerated investment tax writeoffs. Increased efforts to diffuse such publicly supported inventions need to be made. A raising of the savings ratio should be encouraged by tax exempting interest income from so-called thrift accounts, paying interest on checking accounts, encouraging competition within the banking and finance industries (as occurred after 1 January 1980), and various efforts to "conserve" scarce domestic resources. These efforts include raising gasoline, oil, natural gas, and other prices hitherto more or less controlled.

5. Price and wage support programs should be terminated or at least drastically revised downwards.

6. Antitrust actions directed against both implicit and explicit collusion on prices should be encouraged.

7. Large firms in the United States should be permitted to fail (as well as succeed), and their assets purchased at auction by willing buyers. The extension of subsidies to ailing firms should be eliminated.

8. Export and import restrictions in the form of tariffs or quotas should be reduced gradually.

9. Direct commission-type economic (but not safety) regulation should be sharply reduced, as has currently happened in transportation, communications, and banking.

10. Non-industry-specific regulations regarding health, safety, environment, and discrimination should be required to show cost-effectiveness— i.e., the benefits should exceed the costs of specific rulings.

11. Mandatory wage and price controls and guidelines should be a legally sanctioned presidential option, but with strong assurances that the former will not be invoked until the latter have proved a failure, with appropriate sanctions (i.e., federal government refusal to buy from firms violating the guidelines).

12. Experimentation with TIPS and indexation of tax brackets should be encouraged.

The above proposals are relatively nonspecific, but they at least comprise a sort of "agenda for reform," emphasizing that where the competitive outcome is feasible, suitably constrained to insure that external costs are internalized, it is the preferred option. There is still plenty of room for policy activism and initiatives. Indeed, designing the specifics of such a program allows scope for implementation of sociopolitical objectives and values.

In the context of inflation, there is no free lunch. There are, however, a set of options whose costs may be compatible with reducing the pains inflicted by lowering the overall rate of inflation to more politically, socially, and morally compatible levels within the context of American ideals of equality and freedom. As my colleague Harvey Bunke put it, "it is really a matter of the American soul—and therein lies the problem."[23]

8 Epilogue: Supply-Side Economics

Since writing the foregoing, a new phrase, or buzz-word, has confused many and captured the imagination of a few. This concept is also presumed to underlie the economic proposals of the Reagan administration. Much of chapter 4 dealt with the rise and apparent, though not real, decline of demand-side (i.e., Keynesian) economics; let us now examine what is loosely referred to as supply-side economics.

Any new president enters office with a package of more or less specific economic proposals. Thus we have had "Nixonomics," "Carternomics," and so on. These are not based on different economic theories but reflect political-economic choices that the incumbent feels are necessary to tackle actual or anticipated economic conditions. Furthermore, the proposed packages will inevitably be altered by Congress and will not necessarily coincide with what was originally intended. I will not, however, discuss so-called Reagan economics here. Rather, this epilogue will examine the ingredients of supply-side economics from the point of view of an apolitical observer-economist.

Supply-side economics concentrates on providing incentives to increase the productive capacity of the economy. In general, this approach to economic policy aims to increase the quality and quantity of society's productive resources and their more effective exploitation or use. This contrasts with demand-side economics which, in part at least, assumed an ever-increasing capacity to produce in terms of a growing labor force and capital stock, both of increased efficiency. As such, demand-side economics sought to ensure that such growing capacity was adequately used, by attempting to control total spending, to prevent persistent excess capacity or inflationary pressures (as is emphasized in chapters 3 and 4).

Supply-side economics is therefore more long-run in nature while demand-side economics is short-run. The issue of supply-side economics from a policy standpoint is how to augment the nation's productive capacity. Demand-side economics sought, by use of monetary and fiscal policy, to ensure that aggregate demand was held close to the level of assumed capacity. The problems of achieving the latter (chapter 4) have in large part led to renewed emphasis on the former.

How is it possible to enhance the productive capacity of an economy? Supply-siders emphasize the need to increase the rewards to those engaged in productive activity. The stress is thus on tax *reductions*, even in an inflationary era. Such measures are believed to call forth an increased output of goods and services of such a magnitude as to offset inflation and reduce public sector deficits. At the same time, cutting back nonproductive public spending and reducing both the relative size of the federal government and its role in the economy is advocated. "Get the government off the backs of business" is a central theme. The federal government is viewed not as the solution of the problem but as a large part of the problem itself.

Specifically, supply-siders advocate the following:

1. Reduction in the rate of personal income taxation in an across-the-board fashion. The proportionate reduction in marginal tax rates for all income classes is believed to stimulate people to work harder (since take-home pay will have risen) and to induce more people to enter the labor force in view of the greater incentives involved. Thus, both the quality and quantity of labor will increase. This will improve productivity, moderate wage demands, and reduce the inflation rate. The underlying assumption is that workers rationally calculate at the margin the tradeoffs between leisure and after-tax income. An increase in the latter will reduce the former. A reduction in personal income taxes is one route to this believed-to-be desirable result.

In addition, an across-the-board personal income tax reduction will more positively affect household savings than a tax package aimed at giving relatively higher tax benefits to the poor than to the rich. The latter save more absolutely and relatively than the former. Since an increase in savings is needed to finance a noninflationary expansion of productive capital formation, such an increase should also reduce interest rates, thereby giving a further incentive to investment. Income tax changes designed to reduce after-tax income inequality, assist the poor, and so on, have the effect of raising consumption more than savings. The tax structure and level is not to be used to implement social policy but, rather, to stimulate output—not to reduce after-tax inequality but to stimulate incentives to produce, the benefits of which will sooner or later "trickle down" to the deserving poor and reduce both unemployment and inflation.

2. A reduction in business taxes. Similar arguments are advanced as

noted above, namely, that expected after-tax profitability of any given investment will rise and with it the volume of investment. Increased investment will lead to higher productivity and on improved quality of the nation's capital stock as the new investments incorporate the latest technology.

Business taxes may be reduced in several ways. The corporate profit tax rate might be reduced or the allowable rate of depreciation of assets increased. The latter strategy is being pushed by the Reagan administration rather than the former, presumably because a similar policy worked successfully in 1964 (the Kennedy tax package implemented by the Johnson administration).

3. A reduction of the role of the federal government. This aspect of supply-side economics takes two separate forms. One is designed to reduce the share of such expenditures as a proportion of GNP. Acknowledging that, in the short run, significant tax reduction will reduce government revenues (although Laffer-curve enthusiasts dispute this), a reduction in government spending is deemed necessary to prevent a sharp short-run increase in the deficit. The latter, if financed by new money creation, is deemed to be directly inflationary. If not financed by an increase in the money supply, the increased federal government borrowing will raise interest rates and "crowd out" some private investment. In any case, if the economy is operating close to capacity, a bigger deficit will raise aggregate spending and adversely affect inflation.

The second aspect of the reduced role of government is significantly to modify and eliminate large elements of its "interference" in the economy. Three general types of interference with market forces may be identified, namely: direct economic regulation of specific industries by a regulatory commission which controls entry, approves or disallows proposed prices or rates, tries to ensure a fair return on a fair value of the assets and so on; non-industry-specific regulations associated with pollution, discrimination, consumer safety, worker health and safety, etc.; and, finally, direct control of, or support for, specific prices such as oil, natural gas, and various agricultural products.

The first of these measures is represented by the old line regulatory agencies such as the Interstate Commerce Commission and its regulation of railroads, trucks, barges, and pipelines; the Civil Aeronautics Board; the Federal Communications Commission; the Federal Reserve System and its control of banking; etc. The second is represented by the generally newer agencies created since 1960 in response to environmental problems—agencies such as the Environmental Protection Agency, the (much earlier) Food and Drug Administration, the Occupational Safety and Health Administration, the Equal Employment and Opportunities Commission, etc.

The belief is that all of these agencies have imposed costs on businesses far in excess of any social benefits (as discussed in chapter 4). The policy orientation is thus to reduce the degree of administrative interference with market forces by either eliminating some of the agencies, cancelling some of their administrative rulings, or subjecting both past and present rulings to a rigorous benefit-cost test.

In cases where the federal government directly controls prices, the thrust is to eliminate these over time and let market forces prevail, as in the case of oil and natural gas.

4. Stimulation of savings. National savings consist of three components: savings of households (disposable household income less consumption expenditures), savings of business (retained income plus depreciation), and savings of governments (federal, state, and local government surplus or deficit). The across-the-board personal tax reductions are designed to stimulate savings of households directly. Other suggestions are to exempt the first $1,000 or $2,000 of interest income to households. Accelerated depreciation should increase business savings, and the overall tax cuts cum reduction in federal government spending *may* raise total government savings or reduce the deficit.

In general, supply-side economics reverts to the late-eighteenth- and nineteenth-century classical economics. The overall intent is eminently laudable—to create a climate that encourages hard work, thrift, and enterprise, a climate that rekindles the presumably flagging spirit that propelled the Western market-oriented economies to the highest income and output per capita in human history. Even Karl Marx, who was not enamored of the enterprise system as a whole, praised its productive accomplishments: "The bourgeoisie, during its rule of scarce one hundred years, has created more massive and more colossal productive forces than have all preceding generations together."

Limiting the role of the federal government, though expanding the role of state and local governments to pick up the slack, is supposed to unleash entrepreneurial spirits and accelerate real output growth. The various tax incentives are expected to induce such a growth of output that federal deficits will be reduced, not increased, especially when coupled with sharp expenditure reductions in many areas.

This is pretty heady stuff and obviously popular. Who could quarrel with getting government off our backs? Or with reduced taxation, enhanced efficiency, and so on? Yet there are serious analytical as well as political difficulties with each of the above-noted policy thrusts that need to be squarely faced in any assessment of supply-side economics.

First, the across-the-board tax reduction will clearly raise consumption expenditures far more than savings, especially in an inflationary context. Well over 90% of each dollar of increased take-home pay due to the tax reduction will go to consumption, which will raise aggregate demand sharply. This would enhance inflationary trends and expectations. Nor is it clear that higher take-home pay would call forth much more productive effort. Various studies of the effects of taxation on the available labor supply have been made in the United States and elsewhere where tax rates are much higher. The results of such empirical analyses are ambiguous, but at best the effects are minor. Indeed, a rise in real take-home pay may induce less productive effort since many households could then maintain their current standard of living with fewer hours of work per week or per year. In fact, if the real take-home pay of the principal income earner for a family is *reduced*, other family members may be induced or required to enter the labor force to maintain living standards—just the opposite of the supply-side argument.

The reduction in corporate taxation by either a rate reduction or accelerated depreciation for capital assets only assists already profitable firms. Accelerated depreciation is of greatest benefit to the more capital-intensive firms or industries and does little to help the smaller, high technology firms that many expect to be the vanguard of the future; knowledge-intensive industries will get little stimulus from the current depreciation proposals. Overall, reduced corporate taxation should stimulate total investment and hence, after a lag of several years, raise overall growth and productivity. Until this occurs, however, total federal revenues will decline, especially when combined with personal income tax rate reductions.

Nor is it likely that sufficient federal expenditures can be cut to offset the probable short-run reduction in revenues. Such a reduction would raise the deficit and contribute to inflationary pressures and expectations. These consequences are all the more likely to occur if there is a large expansion in military outlays. Furthermore, much of the basic infrastructure supplied or supported by the federal government is believed to be inadequate for both present and future needs. The seaports on both coasts are incapable of accommodating the large coal tankers which are needed to increase coal exports to Europe and Japan. The highway system is viewed as seriously undermaintained as many states have retrenched during the relatively stagnant seventies. The railway right-of-way has long been deteriorated, thus inhibiting cheap, fast, efficient transportation—despite a large amount of federal loan guarantees for refurbishing trackage. Thus more, not less, outlays on such infrastructure so essential to the commerce of the United States is well justified. Similar comments apply to schools and hospitals, even in a supply-side sense, since future economic growth requires a well-educated and healthy labor force.

On the issues of deregulation, much progress has already been made in terms of industry-specific regulation. The Civil Aeronautics Board is scheduled to be phased out in the next few years. Railways, trucks, and banking were substantially deregulated in 1980, and the communications industry has had its detailed regulations sharply curtailed. Natural gas and oil prices are being deregulated. In these areas, there is little or no dispute between supply- or demand-siders. Wherever competition is viewed as at least workably competitive, the market-oriented solution is generally agreed to be preferable. This would also logically entail elimination of import restrictions.

In the area of non-industry-specific regulation, the case is much more controversial, as discussed in the concluding sections of chapter 4. To be sure, policies requiring more rigorous cost effectiveness or cost-benefit analysis of past or future environmental (and other) regulations have much appeal. But there are serious problems in quantifying the costs, and especially the benefits, of unit reductions in pollution from specific emissions. The area of discrimination creates even more measurement difficulties.

Thus, while supply-side economics has great potential for attacking the stagflation problem, it is obviously no cure-all. Its various assumptions have yet to be tested empirically. More federal government spending could well be justified on education and health as well as on basic research and development and other areas of infrastructure. Nor can the demand-side be ignored. Increased capacity to produce requires that overall demand be raised accordingly, lest we have idle men and machines.

Supply-side economics is not new—only the current emphasis thereon is. This concept deserves a fair test, however, but only in the context of sensible monetary and fiscal policies, as noted in chapter 7. Indeed, much of the supply-side rhetoric is based on faith. As one of President Reagan's top economic advisors put it, his optimism is based on his "gut feeling" that everything will turn out all right.

The economy needs—and, indeed, regularly has gotten—both supply-

Notes

2. INFLATION HISTORICALLY REVISITED

1. See the appended footnote by O. Smeaton in Edward Gibbon, *The Decline and Fall of the Roman Empire*, Vol. 1 (New York: Modern Library, Random House, no date) p. 334, f.n. 105.
2. Ibid.
3. A. H. Jones, "Inflation Under the Roman Empire," *Economic History Review*, 2nd series, No. 3, 1953, p. 299.
4. Anna J. Schwartz, "Secular Price Change in Historical Perspective," *The Journal of Money, Credit, and Banking*, February 1973, p. 246.
5. See, however, figure 2.1 below, in which a remarkable price index extending from 1264 to 1960 for southern England is examined.
6. Schwartz, p. 247.
7. Henri Pirenne, *Economic and Social History of Medieval Europe* (New York: Harcourt, Brace & Co., 1937), p. 193.
8. Sir John Clapham, *A Concise Economic History of England* (Cambridge University Press, 1949), p. 119.
9. Schwartz, p. 250 (table 3); J. D. Gould, "The Price Revolution Reconsidered," *Economic History Review*, 2nd Series, December 1964, p. 250; Clapham, pp. 186–87 (in which index numbers are offered).
10. George A. Moore's translation of *Jean Bodin's Response (1568-78) to Malestroit's Paradoxes (1566)*, (Chevy Chase, Md.: The Country Dollar Press), p. 18.
11. Gould, p. 251.
12. Between 1542 and 1547, about £400,000 worth of silver coin was reminted into £526,000 worth of coin, each piece of which contained less than half the previous quantity of pure silver—Henry VIII is reputed to have made a gross profit of £227,000 on the operation. (S. T. Bindoff, *Tudor England* [Baltimore, Md.: Pelican Books, 1950], p. 118). The English pound fell sharply in terms of other currencies. On the eve of the great debasement, it exchanged for 27 Flemish shillings. By 1547, it had fallen to 21; it fell further (to 15) by May 1551, when the English coin was further debased. The currency was not reformed until 1559–60 under Queen Elizabeth.
13. The English money supply is believed to have increased from £848,000 in 1542 to £2,171,000 by July 1551. It declined sharply thereafter. (J. D. Gould, *The Great Debasement* [Oxford, 1970], pp. 81–82).
14. The best estimates are that during the decade 1531–40 Spain "imported" 86.2 million grams of silver and 14.5 million grams of gold. Decade by decade, silver imports rose sharply to over 1,118.6 million grams (1571–80), reaching a peak of 2,707.6 million grams during 1591–1600. They remained above 2,000 million grams until 1631–40, dwindling to 443.4 between 1651

and 1660. (Earl Hamilton, *American Treasure and the Price Revolution in Spain* [Cambridge, Mass.: Harvard University Press, 1934]).

15. The story in other countries is similar, though comparable data continuity is not available.
16. Schwartz, p. 257 (table 5).
17. R. G. Lipsey, "Does Money Always Depreciate?" *Lloyds Bank Review*, October 1960, p. 10.
18. Schwartz, p. 257 (table 5).
19. Lipsey, p. 10; italics in original.
20. D. L. Huddle, "Review Article: Essays on the Economy of Brazil," *Economic Development and Cultural Change*, April 1972, p. 560.
21. Werner Baer, *The Brazilian Economy: Its Growth and Development* (Columbus, Ohio: Grid Publishing Co., 1979), p. 62.
22. For details, see ibid., chapter 4.
23. There are various price indexes; the above refer to the internal price index and the implicit GDP deflator. See Baer, p. 173 (table 37).
24. The combination of high rates of inflation and sluggish real growth of output, with its consequent high unemployment rates, is often referred to as "stagflation." (See chapter 3.)
25. Baer, p. 94.
26. W. Baer and P. Becherman, "The Trouble with Index-Linking: Reflections on the Recent Brazilian Experience," *World Development*, Vol. 8, 1980, Table 1, p. 680.
27. Ibid., p. 101 (table 27).
28. "Indexation" is defined and discussed further in chapter 7.
29. Devaluation of any currency means the increasing of the official number of units of a country's currency that will exchange for the currency of other countries—usually the U.S. dollar, or gold where the gold standard prevails. Thus, if initially 5 pesos were deemed to be the equivalent of one U.S. dollar (in the sense that dealers in foreign exchange would trade at the 5 to 1 ratio), a devaluation of 20% would require 6 pesos to purchase $1. The dollar is said to have *appreciated* in this instance, and the peso to have *depreciated* or become devalued.
30. GDP refers to gross domestic product. Like the more familiar GNP (gross national product), it is a measure of the value of total national production during a given time period, usually one year.
31. Baer & Becherman, p. 700.
32. Ibid., p. 701.
33. *Wall Street Journal*, 19 December 1980, p. 20. For some of the disadvantages of indexing, see the discussion in chapter 7 below.
34. Frank D. Graham, *Exchange, Prices, and Production in Hyper-Inflation: Germany, 1920–1923* (Princeton, New Jersey: Princeton University Press, 1930), p. 13.
35. Ibid., p. 56.
36. Ibid., p. 13.
37. Nathan Guttman and Patricia Meehan, *The Great Inflation* (England: Saxon House, 1975), p. x.
38. Ibid., p. 4.
39. Graham, p. 7.
40. Ibid., p. 16.
41. Karsten Laursen and Jorgen Pedersen, *The German Inflation 1918–1923* (Amsterdam: North-Holland Publishing Company, 1964), p. 53.

42. Ibid., p. 52.
43. It should be noted that the government took action in 1920 to increase tax revenues and, for a while, tax revenues did actually increase between April 1920 and March 1921. (Ibid., p. 34.)
44. Guttman and Meehan, pp. 20–21.
45. Graham, p. 30.
46. Ibid., p. 66.
47. Ibid., p. 65.
48. Guttman and Meehan, p. 30.
49. Ibid., p. 30; Laursen and Pedersen, pp. 79–80.
50. Laursen and Pedersen, p. 123.
51. Guttman and Meehan, p. 223.
52. Philip Cagan, "The Monetary Dynamics of Hyperinflation" in M. Friedman, ed., *Studies in the Quantity Theory of Money* (Chicago: University of Chicago Press, 1956), p. 26 (table 3).
53. The World Bank, *World Development Report, 1980* (Oxford: Oxford University Press, 1980), pp. 110–111 (table 1).
54. Ibid.
55. The longing for security in Germany, a legacy of the catastrophic experience of the hyperinflation, "determined the attitude of many Germans." And when the Great Depression unexpectedly struck, it "confronted them with new problems and choices. They chose Hitler." (Guttman and Meehan, p. 239.)

3. CAUSES OF INFLATION

1. In 1933, for example, the unemployment rate was 24.9% and in 1975, only 8.5%.
2. Some transfer payment changes occur automatically. Thus, when unemployment rises, unemployment compensation in total also rises, thus maintaining incomes and hence expenditures at levels higher than would otherwise exist. In inflationary times, with social security and some wages indexed, income payments also increase, with similar effects on total spending—which, of course, aggravates an excess demand inflation.
3. For example, if the sum of the two rates was 10%, then to reduce the inflation rate to 4% would imply a 6% unemployment rate. Any other combination of inflation and unemployment rates adding to 10% was possible, if the sum of the two could be viewed as constant.
4. One measure of this inverse relationship concluded that "according to this empirical trade-off relation, maintaining an unemployment rate of 4% eventually leads to an inflation rate of 4% as well. A 6% unemployment rate, if maintained, would be accompanied by an inflation rate of only 1.7%." (S. Hymans, "The Inflation-Unemployment Trade-off: Theory and Experience," in W. Smith and R. Teigen [eds.], *Readings in Money, National Income, and Stabilization Policy* [Homewood, Ill.: Irwin, 1974].)
5. Citibank *Monthly Letter*, October 1979, p. 7.
6. For some details, see ibid., pp. 6–9.
7. On a monthly basis, in fact, since June 1980, the unemployment rate for adult females has been equal to or below that of adult males, signaling a significant shift in the impact of increasing female participation rates.
8. For some details, see P. O. Flaim, "The Effect of Demographic Changes on the Nation's Unemployment Rate" in National Commission on Employ-

ment and Unemployment Statistics, *Counting the Labor Force*, Appendix, Volume III, pp. 192–193, Washington, D.C., December 1979, and references cited therein.

9. Ibid.

10. K. W. Clarkson and R. E. Meiners, "Inflated Unemployment Statistics," *Law and Economics Center*, University of Miami School of Law, March 1977.

11. Flaim, p. 196.

12. See Flaim, p. 198, for a summary.

13. Phillip Cagan, *The Hydra-Headed Monster: The Problem of Inflation in the U.S.*, 1974, p. 6.

14. Arthur M. Okun, "The Invisible Handshake and the Inflationary Process," *Challenge*, January/February 1980, pp. 5–12.

15. Lester Thurow, *Generating Inequality* (New York: Basic Books, Inc., 1975), especially chapters 4 and 5.

16. *Annual Report of the Council of Economic Advisers*, January 1980, Washington, D.C., p. 75.

17. Ibid., pp. 75–76.

18. See chapter 1.

19. Gottfried Haberler, *Inflation: Its Causes and Cures* (Washington, D.C.: American Enterprise Institute for Public Policy Research, July 1966), p. 3.

4. THE ROLE OF GOVERNMENT

1. These were needed because deliberate, conscious policy initiatives in the Keynesian spirit were not tried in the United States until the so-called Kennedy tax reduction of 1964. Other Western democracies used monetary and fiscal policy more deliberately and effectively much earlier.

2. A good, lively and concise survey of the economy during the 1930s, '40s, '50s, and early '60s is provided in John P. Lewis and Robert C. Turner, *Business Conditions Analysis*, 2nd ed., 1967, Part Three, pp. 291–360.

3. For some fascinating details of Federal Reserve policy during the period of the Great Depression, see Milton Friedman and Anna J. Schwartz, *A Monetary History of the United States, 1867–1960* (Princeton: Princeton University Press, 1963), chapter 7, "The Great Contraction, 1929–33."

4. Friedman has reported that this was only part of his statement and that it misrepresented his views. The full quotation is as follows: "In one sense, we are all Keynesians now; in another, no one is a Keynesian any longer." (Milton Friedman, *Dollars and Deficits* [Englewood Cliffs, N.J.: Prentice Hall, 1968], p. 15.)

5. Even President Nixon once billed himself as a "Keynesian" in the early 1970s.

6. Walter W. Heller, *New Dimensions of Political Economy* (Cambridge, Mass.: Harvard University Press, 1966), pp. 59–60.

7. J. M. Keynes, *The General Theory of Employment, Interest and Money* (London: Macmillan, 1951), p. 380.

8. In a similar fashion, changing the money supply growth to accommodate commerce, aggravates rather than offsets instability.

9. Some of the better known models are those of the Bureau of Economic Analysis (U.S. Department of Commerce), the Brookings Institution, Data

Resources, Inc., the Federal Reserve Bank of St. Louis, the MIT-Penn Social Science Research Council, the Federal Reserve Board, Wharton Econometric Forecasting Associates, and many others.

10. For a discussion, see Michael K. Evans, "The Bankruptcy of Keynesian Econometric Models," *Challenge*, January/February 1980.

11. *Annual Report of the Council of Economic Advisers*, January 1966, pp. 31–32.

12. Murray Weidenbaum in *Economic Effects of Vietnam Spending*, Hearings before the Joint Economic Committee, Vol. 1 (Washington, D.C.: Government Printing Office, 1967), pp. 209–10. Italics in original.

13. See Charles E. McLure, Jr., in Cagan, Estey, Fellner, McLure, and Moore, *Economic Policy and Inflation in the Sixties* (Washington, D.C.: American Enterprise Institute, 1972), pp. 42–43.

14. However, there was a reversal of auto and telephone excise tax cuts and a speedup in corporation tax payments and graduated income tax withholding.

15. *Annual Report of the Council of Economic Advisers*, January 1967, p. 46.

16. Heller, pp. 87–88.

17. A lively account of the struggle to get the surcharge is given in Lyndon Baines Johnson, *The Vantage Point* (New York: Holt, Rinehart and Winston, 1971), chapter 19.

18. *Annual Report of the Council of Economic Advisers*, January 1973, p. 82.

19. For a lively account, see John M. Blair, *The Control of Oil* (New York: Vintage Books, 1978), chapter 11.

20. For other details, see table 4-1.

21. *Annual Report of the Council of Economic Advisers*, January 1980, p. 61.

22. It has been estimated that a subterranean economy exists in the United States of considerable dimension and growing very rapidly. Illegal transactions, for example, are not counted as part of GNP. The evidence is that prostitution and drug traffic in the United States and elsewhere involve perhaps hundreds of billions of dollars each year. Many other types of transactions, all involving economic activity, never get recorded, such as baby-sitters' services or bartering of services to avoid high taxes and social security payments.

23. Otto Eckstein, "Economic Choices for the 1980's," *Challenge*, July/August 1980, p. 25.

24. For some details regarding the intercity freight industries, see George W. Wilson, *Economic Analysis of Intercity Freight Transportation* (Bloomington, Indiana: Indiana University Press, 1980), chapter 4.

25. For a generally negative evaluation of OSHA along these lines, see Robert S. Smith, *The Occupational Safety and Health Act* (Washington, D.C.: American Enterprise Institute, 1976).

26. *Wall Street Journal*, 9 July 1980, p. 4.

27. *Time*, 26 March 1979, p. 63.

28. There is much rhetoric and controversy concerning the benefits that society receives from these costs, especially those associated with the "newer" agencies. A summary of several of the recent empirical estimates of benefits concludes that, on the whole, they have proven cost-effective. That is, the benefits exceed the costs. There are, of course, enormous measurement problems for both the benefit and cost sides, and no one would argue that every administrative ruling, limitation on emissions, or hiring quota is cost-effec-

tive. Yet, overall, this appears to be the case. (See Wm. K. Tabb, "Government Regulations: Two Sides to the Story," *Challenge*, November/December 1980.)

29. Thus, for example, the Carter Administration announced new price supports on 29 July 1980, raising them from $4.50 to $5.02 per bushel of soybeans, from $2.50 to $3.00 per bushel for wheat, etc. (*Wall Street Journal*, 29 July 1980, p. 3). The proximity of this announcement to the November election is to be noted.

30. Certain states have such agencies as Alcoholic Beverage Commissions that specify prices for these products, thereby eliminating price competition. The overall effect is trivial, but the annoyance factor substantial.

5. THE ROLE OF MONEY

1. Earlier, the Fed agreed to make available the minutes of its meetings, but only after an interval of time.

2. Friedman and Schwartz, p. 14.

3. This discrepancy is partly caused by the fact that the $206 billion annual figure is the mid-year estimate (June) while the $217 billion figure refers to December. The Friedman-Schwartz figure for December 1960 is $211 billion. Also, between January and August, 1959, the series was expanded to include data for banks in Alaska and Hawaii. Other, though minor, discrepancies remain.

4. T. D. Simpson, "The Redefined Monetary Aggregates," *Federal Reserve Bulletin*, February 1980.

5. Ibid., p. 97.

6. *Economic Indicators July, 1980*, prepared for the Joint Economic Committee by the Council of Economic Advisers (Washington, D.C.: U.S. Government Printing Office, 1980), pp. 26–27.

7. Any good elementary text in economics will provide the mechanical details and some of the complications.

8. Thomas Mun, *England's Treasure by Foreign Trade* (circa 1630) extracted in L. D. Abbott, ed., *Masterworks of Economics*, Vol. 1, McGraw Hill Paperback Ed., 1963, p. 6.

9. I mention Hume specifically because some recent monetarists have attributed much of their position to that of Hume. The search for ancestors of any position is never-ending, as if that gives the position some special stature. (See Thomas Mayer, "David Hume and Monetarism," *Quarterly Journal of Economics*, August 1980.)

10. See *The 1980 Midyear Review of the Economy: the Recession and the Recovery*, Report of the Joint Economic Committee, Congress of the United States (Washington, D.C.: U.S. Government Printing Office, 1980).

11. Ibid., p. 13.

12. Milton Friedman, *The Counter-Revolution in Monetary Theory* (London: Institute of Economic Affairs, 1970), p. 16.

13. Ibid., p. 23.

14. Ibid., pp. 23–24. During the decade of the 1950s in Brazil, for example, there was a very rapid increase in the money supply, which mainly affected ouput rather than prices. After this period, further money supply increases influenced prices primarily. (See chapter 2.)

15. Using M1, this ratio varied from a low of .95 in 1968 to a high of 3.66 in

1963. Using M2, the ratio fluctuated between a low of .81 in 1968 to a high of 2.08 in 1969.

16. Data on M1, CPI, GNP deflator, and real GNP have been converted into index numbers, with 1967 = 100 for each series. Data from *Annual Report of the Council of Economic Advisers*, 1979.

17. I refer to such developments as Samuelson's interaction of the accelerator and multipliers, Harrod's "razor's edge," as well as to the earlier work of Schumpeter, Kondratieff, plus a host of business cycle theorists, to say nothing of secular stagnation based on a simplified consumption function.

6. THE CONSEQUENCES OF INFLATION

1. Of course, during the 1970s many other uncertainty-enhancing events occurred, such as the energy situation, other supply-side shocks, persistent instability in countries supplying needed resources, and so on. These also contributed to inflation as well as being independent sources of increased uncertainty.

2. E. Budd and D. Seiders, "The Impact of Inflation on the Distribution of Income and Wealth," *The American Economic Review*, May 1971, pp. 134–35.

3. G. L. Bach and J. B. Stephenson, "Inflation and the Redistribution of Wealth," *The Review of Economics and Statistics*, February 1974, pp. 1–2.

4. Regardless of these aggregate changes in relative shares, there is no warrant to suggest from such evidence that the poor do not suffer disproportionately from high rates of inflation. If the prices of the goods and services purchased by the poor and the elderly rise faster than the overall index (i.e., the "necessities"), then welfare or pension payments must rise faster to prevent a deterioration in real purchasing power. Aggregative data also hide such widely believed facts that prices in ghetto areas rise faster and/or are higher than elsewhere.

5. E. Nowotny, "Inflation and Taxation: Reviewing the Macroeconomic Issues," *Journal of Economic Literature*, September 1980, p. 1039.

6. J. H. Minarik, "Who Wins, Who Loses from Inflation," *Challenge*, January/February 1979, p. 27.

7. The Fed, commercial banks, and savings institutions always "repay" in precisely the same nominal amounts, which, with rising prices, have lower purchasing power.

8. Bach and Stephenson, p. 3.

9. This is largely a guess—but based on the above-mentioned study and given the much higher inflation rates of the 1970s.

10. Ibid., p. 4.

11. Ibid., p. 5.

12. Ibid.

13. Ibid., p. 13.

7. CURES FOR INFLATION

1. *Annual Report of the Council of Economic Advisers* (Washington, D.C.: U.S. Government Printing Office, 1976), pp. 20–21.

2. The hourly rate for baby-sitting in my area of the country still hovers about

$1.00, unchanged in 20 years. Crude estimates suggest that prices are 20–40% lower than in the "observed sector" (*Wall Street Journal*, 20 October 1980, p. 1).

3. Ibid.

4. Recently, Chrysler, Braniff International, Firestone, General Motors, Wheeling-Pittsburgh Steel, and Uniroyal have negotiated reduced pay and/or benefits with their employees in order to keep the companies solvent and preserve jobs. For example, employees at Uniroyal "took a cut of 58 cents an hour for the last five months of 1980, and agreed to forego living-cost raises due in July and October, plus part of the January 1981 living-cost increase" (*Wall Street Journal*, 22 October 1980, p. 27).

5. Arthur Okun, "Efficient Disinflationary Policies," *The American Economic Review, Papers and Proceedings*, May 1978, p. 348.

6. See below for a discussion of wage-price *controls*, as well as wage-price *guidelines*.

7. See chapter 2, pp. 13–20.

8. The value of a bond yielding an income stream of, say, $1,000 per period is $1,000 divided by the interest rate. If the interest rate were 3%, the value of the bond (i.e., its price in a competitive bond market) would be $33,333 $\left(\frac{\$1,000}{0.03}\right)$.

   If prices rose by 10% and the purchasing power of the nominal $1,000 was to be preserved, this income would rise to $1100 per period. But if the "real" interest rate of 3% were to be preserved, the nominal interest rate would be 13%. Thus, the value (price) of the bond would plummet to $8462 $\left(\frac{\$1,000}{0.13}\right)$. If, at the same time, the value of the bonds were indexed, its price would rise to about $36,666. No one, however, would pay this amount to receive a nominal income of $1100 per period at a nominal interest rate of $13%.

9. See Herman Kahn and Irving Levenson, "How Not to Index the Economy," *Fortune*, 17 November 1980, p. 64. The case is similar for business borrowing for investment purposes.

10. Ibid.

11. *Annual Report of the Council of Economic Advisers* (Washington, D.C.: U.S. Government Printing Office, 1962), p. 185.

12. Ibid., p. 189.

13. *Annual Report of the Council of Economic Advisers*, 1972, p. 108.

14. *In Pursuit of Price Stability: The Wage-Price Freeze of 1971* (Washington, D.C.: The Brookings Institution, 1973), p. 39.

15. C. L. Schultze, "Why Controls Don't Work," *Wall Street Journal*, 27 February 1980, p. 20.

16. "The Case for Wage-Price Controls," *Wall Street Journal*, 27 February 1980, p. 20.

17. Lester Thurow, "The U.S. Productivity Problem," Data Resources *Review*, August 1979.

18. *Annual Report of the Council of Economic Advisers* (Washington, D.C.: U.S. Government Printing Office, January 1980), p. 84 and table 15.

19. John W. Kendrick, *Understanding Productivity* (Baltimore, Md.: The Johns Hopkins University Press, 1977), p. 29.

20. Defined as the "trend increase of the cost of the factors of production" or

the wage trend less the productivity trend equals the trend of unit labor cost (Otto Eckstein, *Tax Policy and Core Inflation*, a paper prepared for the Joint Economic Committee, 10 April 1980, p. 6; and Eckstein, "Economic Choices for the 1980's," *Challenge*, July/August 1980, p. 17).

21. This is a much more complicated issue than we have space to analyze further. Clearly, cleaner air, reduced discrimination, safer drugs, toys and consumer products in general, healthier and safer work environment, are "goods." However, it is unclear whether the benefits of such goods, however measured, more than compensate for the costs incurred.

22. Employment increased at the rate of over 2% per year during the 1970s. compared with about half this rate in the 1950s and 1960s.

23. *Business Horizons*, June 1980, p. 8.

Index